Praise

"Business owners often don't have the time and foresight to think about exit planning, and it is one of the most important—and overlooked—aspects of the planning process. Dan's case studies provide valuable insights for today's financial professionals involved in exit planning, while uncovering his wealth of knowledge in the business owner market."
—**John DiMonda, SVP, Head of Lincoln Financial Advisors**

"This book is loaded with great lessons on how to successfully exit your business. It will give you valuable insights that can change your mindset!"
—**Brian Tracy, Author/Speaker/Consultant**

"For business owners and those who professionally serve them, Dan Prisciotta takes you on a journey that will open your heart and mind to the importance of getting your exit right for your and the next generations of your family."
—**John Marshall, Founding Partner, The Resource Group**

"As a successor of a family business, one thing I know well is that business owners are subject-matter experts. They live and breathe their businesses. However, when it comes to business planning, there are many outside and interconnected issues (legal, tax, creditor, financial, etc.) that are foreign to the business owner. Bringing in a quarterback with their team of experts allows the business owner to know the opportunities and challenges. From selling for the highest dollar to making sure those dollars aren't lost to excessive taxation, while utilizing a time-tested process with a team of advisors, is critical to making the process both efficient and controllable to the business owner, the backbone of our country." —**Matthew Roberson, CFP®, CBEC®, Partner, C Solutions**

"Dan's expertise and guidance through the process made it a wonderful experience for all." —**Tara L. Blair, CPA*, CFP®, Business Intelligence Institute Specialist**

"Equity Strategies Group has been an invaluable resource for our financial advisors and their business-owner clients. ESG's bench strength, access to industry specialists, and deep desire to help the privately held business owner is what sets it apart. Thanks Dan and the ESG team for all you do in the business owner marketplace. You are a treasure!" —**Nathan Truax, Director of Advisor Development, LFA and CEO of Business Transfer Consultants**

"I've known Dan for almost 20 years, and he has been one of the top financial professionals at Lincoln Financial Advisors' elite think tank, The Resource Group. He has shared valuable insights with both his peers and clients, and is well-respected throughout the organization for his knowledge of business owner exit strategies. I recommend you read his new book!" —**Pete Giaccio, Chief Executive of The Resource Group**

"The ESG team is an excellent resource for my business-owner clients. They have time-tested, proven processes to help business owners develop exit plans and then execute them with confidence. Most importantly, they take the time to get to know each business owner's unique situation. I had a business owner tell me that he was impressed with ESG's professionalism and timeliness, but most of all the fact that adding ESG to his exit team made him feel like he was going through the process with a group of trusted friends that genuinely cared about the outcome and the effects it would have on him and his family. Working with ESG is always an enriching experience for both my clients and my practice!" —Paul J. Meyer, CEPA, CBEC, CRPC, Sagemark Consulting

"Quite frankly, without ESG, my client would have been forced into liquidation. The years of love and care for their business and employees would have been dissolved. Unfortunate circumstances created the need to sell. Not only did ESG bring initial strategies to the table, but when circumstances changed again, ESG was quickly able to pivot and find the right solution. My clients have maintained the company (with new owners) and protected jobs while gaining financial security. Simply put, ESG is a fantastic resource to have in my business exit and succession toolkit." —Michael A. Cohen, CRPC, CEBC, Sagemark Consulting

"Who doesn't love a good story? Well, you're in for a treat because these are 17 GREAT stories in this book! You can tell from these case studies that Dan has "been there, done that," and that he's passionate about passing that knowledge and expertise along to others. I also know this from personal experience, having been a colleague of Dan's for about three decades. Equity Strategies Group has been integral in helping our clients achieve the successful exit they had always hoped for. If you love a good story, and are a business owner or advisor—then this is the book for you!" —Dianna Parker, CFP, CBEC, Executive Director, Business Intelligence Institute

"This book is going to smash your existing anxiety about owner exit planning and lay the groundwork for successful succession." —Mark C. Bronfman, MBA, CPA, author of *The Profits Interest*, Founder, Bold Value

"Having worked with Dan for well over 20 years in the most complex and diverse situations imaginable, I can say in complete sincerity and

confidence that there are none better. High praise indeed, but as the executive director for 19 years of a private high-net-worth advisory group, I can confirm that Dan is 'Top of Class.' His subject matter expertise, his compassionate 'bedside manner,' and his ability to advise and guide a client in a trusting, highly productive relationship, above all, is unique and unparalleled. This book illustrates all the tools and techniques while inviting readers into further meaningful, relational connections."
—**Russ Jones, Executive Director of Sagemark Consulting Private Wealth Services**

"*One Way Out—The Case Studies* is a must read for any business owner contemplating an exit from their business...and all owners will eventually exit. You only get one shot at a successful sale. Learn from other owners that have gone through the process and found their One Way Out." —**Michael Palumbos, Host of** *The Family Biz Show,* **Family Wealth Advisor**

"When it came time for my client to exit from his business, I wanted to make sure he had the best team possible around him. I brought in ESG because I knew they would have the right process and resources to help for the transaction. I believe this allowed him to obtain the right value for his company and that's exactly what happened! Now that he is financially independent, I am so proud to say that in a small way I have helped him get there." —**Bruce Charleton, MBA, CLTC®, CBEC®, BII Specialist, The Resource Group**

"Exiting your business is a complex and irreversible endeavor. This compelling book provides a glimpse into 17 business exit case studies that illuminate the financial element of an exit transaction, dove-tailed with the human element. Dan is a true thought leader in this space, so do yourself, your family, and your employees a favor and read this book!"
—**Joseph W. Brezden, CLU®, ChFC®, CFBS, CRPC®, CBEC® & Michael J. Brezden, CFA, Brezden Wealth Advisors**

Contents at a Glance

Foreword

Today's business world is crowded at the top. There's no doubt that major corporations have a strong hold on the American consciousness —and economy.

Yet, despite the prevalence of chains and big names, small businesses remain the backbone of America and are a powerful force that keeps the economic machine running. As of 2021, the United States was home to 32.5 million small businesses (defined as having fewer than 500 employees), making up 99.9% of all U.S. businesses and employing nearly half (47%) of all U.S.-based workers.

Behind these small businesses are everyday people with stories of hard work and sacrifice, success and failure, aspiration and legacy ... and so much more. The people who own these businesses give blood, sweat, and tears to make their dreams a success. When it comes time for owners to exit the business, usually to retire, the process for them is more than a financial decision—it's a life milestone.

This is exactly why *One Way Out-The Case Studies* is so important.

I have spent more than 35 years in the financial services industry. I have learned that the emphasis should not be placed on "financial"—it's about the "service." In other words, how do we, as financial professionals who give advice in life's critical moments, serve the business owners seeking counsel?

It's all about being a leader who is a servant for others, and pairing emotional intelligence with the data-driven financial advice. Small business owners must trust their advisor not only as a professional, but as a friend and confidant. This trust is earned through relationship-building and empathetic listening, demonstrating vulnerability so that owners may feel connected during a life-changing event.

Author Dan Prisciotta understands and believes in the value of servant leadership and empathetic listening for all those seeking financial advice and, critically, America's small business owners. The case studies found within this book will demonstrate how financial professionals and their small business owner clients can harness their relationship to help ensure the best results for everyone involved.

The Lincoln Financial Advisors philosophy—Serve First, Last and Always™—drives the way we do business, with clients' best interests at heart—and I couldn't agree more.

Tim Seifert
Senior Vice President and Head of Retirement Solutions Distribution, Lincoln Financial Distributors

Introduction

"The world seems to belong to those who reach out and grab it with both hands. It belongs to those who do something rather than just wish and hope and plan and pray and intend to do something, when everything is just right." —Brian Tracy

This book is for business owners, and their financial advisors, who want to successfully exit from their company and achieve financial independence and happiness. It is a logical sequel to my popular book *One Way Out: How to Grow, Protect, and Exit from Your Business,* published in 2016. That book provided a foundation of knowledge and described an exit-planning process to help you achieve success. This book embraces that process through real-life case studies highlighting actual exit transactions that my firm, Equity Strategies Group (ESG), and I have completed on behalf of our clients. Of course, names and some other minor elements have been changed to protect confidentiality.

I have found case studies to be the best way to facilitate adult learning and understanding. The events, concepts, and lessons learned are highly transferrable to you whether your business is worth $10 million or over $1 billion. In a relatively brief amount of time, in an interview style of writing, I hope to convey many important concepts you need to know so that you can achieve that same level of confidence, preparedness, and results our clients have experienced. I also want you to avoid making fatal mistakes. You can absorb the small ones, but the big ones will have a devastating impact on you, your business, and your future.

My clients are the most successful people I know. Their courage, grit, intelligence, and determination have helped them start and grow a business. Most founders started with almost nothing. Over the years, their business provided valuable products and services to its customers, created jobs, fueled prosperity, and strengthened our great nation. At some point, the owner(s) of that business will begin to consider their exit strategy. No one gets out of this life alive—100% of owners will exit…either vertically or horizontally! You can procrastinate and react, or you be proactive and create a plan, assemble a team, and execute your preferred strategy so that you leave on your terms, at the right value.

It boils down to evaluating five exit paths to figure out your optimal "One Way Out":

1. Gift or sale to your family
2. Sale to your partner/co-shareholders
3. Sale to "insiders," i.e., your employees or key management team
4. Sale to an outside party such as a strategic (industry) or financial (private equity) buyer
5. Go public (note: very few middle-market companies will do this, for various reasons)

If you are not entirely sure which path to choose, when the right timing is, how to choose a path, or what your business is truly worth, you're not alone. A relatively new profession of "exit planning" has emerged to help you through these critical decisions. Not everyone who labels themselves an exit planner is necessarily qualified to help you. You want an experienced professional who specializes in this type of work or has access to the right team who can help you. The right team has "been there and done that" many times and can lead you through their proven process.

Ideally, you will explore the pros and cons of several exit paths to determine which is best for you. Following these steps will give the best results:

1. Establish your exit goals (to whom? when? how? at what valuation?).
2. Measure your financial and emotional readiness to exit.
3. Learn and choose your optimal exit path and strategy.
4. Understand the value of the option you choose.
5. Execute your exit strategy with your team of advisors to achieve your exit goals and protect your wealth.

Step 5 is the most important; you need execution. A plan without execution is not worth the paper it is written on. What do I mean by execution? Once you decide which exit path, or which "one way out" is right for you and your business, you will need to find a qualified intermediary (investment banker, M&A firm, ESOP specialist, etc.) to help you implement your chosen transaction. They will work with your advisory team to help prepare you and your business to go to market.

Next, you need to create a plan for what your life will look like when you no longer own your business. This is a scary proposition for many owners. Fears, doubts, and anxiety may hold them back. You will go from a world that you know into a world with which you may be less familiar. One aspect of this transition is figuring out how you will attain fulfillment and happiness. The other aspect is achieving and maintaining financial independence and protecting your newly found liquid wealth. Having these formal plans in advance is paramount to a successful exit. This is not a do-it-yourself proposition. Luck is when preparedness meets opportunity. The very act of preparation will help attract what you most desire. A team of experienced professionals, including your financial advisor, exit planning specialists, and transaction intermediaries, along with your accountant and attorney, will help you achieve the best results. When your time comes, develop a plan and a team, and launch!

The flip side to not doing proper planning can be a disastrous outcome. Over the years, I have seen a number of unfortunate situations that resulted from weak or non-existent planning, along with poor decision making (see the following list). As always, you are 100% responsible for the outcome.

- Owner who sold too late. The buyer sensed a desperate seller who held on too long without a plan B, or perhaps the owner simply missed the economic cycle and received a much lower valuation as a result.
- Owner who sold too young and squandered the proceeds without a plan to manage their assets properly.
- Owner who sold directly to a buyer, without an investment banker, left millions of dollars on the table and paid millions in unnecessary income taxes because the transaction structure favored the buyer.
- Owner who did not have proper representation when selling their business and accepted a deferred payment plan but never received final payment and continued to be at risk for business liabilities even after the sale closed.
- Owner who didn't retain an investment banker and accepted the first and only offer she ever received to buy her business. She felt her business was "unique" and this was the best and only possible buyer for the company. We later determined that there were plenty of interested, qualified buyers in the market who would have paid double the price if she had retained an investment banker and ran a competitive auction process.
- Owner who confused a letter of intent (LOI) with an actual purchase offer. An LOI is nonbinding, and the dollar amount is subject to change during the due diligence phase. They did not have a team of professionals to help them prepare for the buyer's due diligence team's onslaught; the LOI was blown up and the offer was reduced by 50%. Both parties walked away in disgust after wasting a lot of time and money.
- Owner who tried to sell her business on their own, not realizing it could take 800 to 1,000 hours or more to complete a transaction. The process dragged on unnecessarily, and they took their eye off the ball, losing several key customers and employees while spending too much time fielding constant inquiries from a potential buyer. That buyer ultimately walked away because the business's key financial

measurement of earnings before interest, taxes, depreciation, and amortization (EBITDA) dropped from $2.5 million in the prior year to under $1 million. If you think investment banking fees are expensive, try losing a deal and having to pick up the pieces.

* Owner who transferred the business to his son and daughter, who were not ready and went bankrupt three years later – not to mention the damage done to the family.
* Owner who sold to four of his key employees, retired to Sarasota, and collected note payments for only two years. The business failed and the key employees defaulted on the note. He was forced to return to work.
* Owner who jumped at an unsolicited offer from a competitor, sold, and was not emotionally prepared for retirement. Without adequate thought and preparation, they experienced seller's remorse and regretted their impulsive sale.
* Owner who sold her business and received an enormous amount of money, and then promptly lost it all by investing in a business with which she was unfamiliar, along with other "sure-fire" private placements, cryptocurrencies, NFTs, and other risky "alternative investments" that "couldn't miss."
* Owner who tried to sell their business with just his CFO's and CPA's guidance, only to waste years talking with the wrong people and not getting a deal done. The emotional damage to the owner and reputational damage done to the business were devasting. Sadly, even if he managed to eventually get a deal done, he would never know how much money he left on the table.
* Owner who decided to sell his company and hired an investment banker, who brought him a number of fully valued, attractive offers. The owner decided that none of the offers were acceptable, and took the company off the market. Shortly thereafter, the owner was diagnosed with a serious medical condition. While undergoing treatment for his medical condition, the owner's attention was distracted away from daily operations of the business, and the

company's performance suffered. The owner passed away a short time later, and the owner's estate sold the business, at a fraction of the value that had previously been offered.

The list goes on and on. You have worked too hard for too long and only have one chance to do this right! I hope this book will protect you from making these all-too-common mistakes.

This book is broken into two sections. The first focuses on sales to outsiders for maximum value. The second focuses on internal transfers—in particular, sales to employee stock ownership plans (ESOPs), which have become extremely popular, and a sale to a company's management team. I have also interspersed sidebars with topics of relevancy to the story to amplify certain points, processes, or technical topics.

My hope is that *One Way Out—The Case Studies* will help educate you about the importance of this type of planning. Once you understand how the lack of a plan can put everything at risk, your thinking may begin to change.

This book also presents examples of how to begin this process without a large commitment of time, money, or other resources through the use of ESG's complimentary Marketability Assessment. This confidential assessment will help you focus on determining which exit path is right for you, how to prepare for your exit, a possible range of values for your business (depending on which path you choose), and what the process looks like (timing, players, costs, etc.). After we deliver the Marketability Assessment, the choice is yours. Our mission is to objectively help you make choices that are best for you, your business, and your family. Our firm's philosophy is to "Serve First, Last, and Always" with your best interests at heart.

10 REASONS BUSINESS OWNERS DECIDE TO EXIT

So how do you know when the time is right for your exit? Your time may be now if one or more of the following resonate with you.

1. **You get tired and burnt out.** You may be at a point where other things are more interesting or appealing than your business. If you wait until you are tired or burnt out, you are already on

the downside of the value curve, as your business may lose vital force and momentum that is critical for the ongoing growth and success necessary to obtain maximum value.

2. **You want to protect against dying prematurely.** To whom will ownership pass? If you own 100% of the company it will pass to your spouse or children. Are they prepared to keep or sell it? If other owners, is there a current buy-sell agreement among owners that will dictate the price and terms of the sale? Is the buyout mandatory or optional? Is the price in the agreement fair based on today's value? Is life insurance in place to provide cash to fund the purchase? Are there appropriate plans in place to ensure a smooth transition, not only of ownership but of leadership as well? Will the company function and survive without you?

3. **A key employee leaves.** Does your business have a highly valued management team or several key employees? Are these key people subject to employment agreements and/or other restrictions? Do you have special incentive compensation plans with "handcuffs," such as vesting schedules, to retain them?

4. **Unsolicited offers come along.** Is the business ready to be sold? Are you financially and emotionally ready for a transaction? Is your personal financial and estate planning up to date? Will acceptance of an offer satisfy all of your needs and desires? Did you run the numbers on your personal after-tax cash flow for the next 20 or 30-plus years, considering various what-ifs? Is it your intention to transfer the business to family members or employees? Does an outside sale make sense?

5. **Business reversals.** Perhaps a company fails to adapt to changing markets (pandemic, supply chain disruption, inflation, threat of recession), competition arises from unexpected quarters, or an accident or bad luck generates substantial losses. Sometimes the affected business never fully recovers and a forced liquidation results.

6. **An owner divorces.** Marital dissolutions can create settlement terms and immediate cash needs that are so onerous that a business needs to be sold to settle the divorce judgement. Emotional stress resulting from divorce may also create the need to sell the business.

7. **Life-changing experiences occur.** The emotional or physical shock of heart attacks, cancer, or close calls with death in accidents sometimes fosters a strong desire for owners to do things differently with the rest of their life and not "die at their desk."

8. **Lack of estate tax planning.** The absence of an up-to-date estate tax plan can precipitate the forced sale of a business if your estate lacks liquidity to pay estate taxes, which can approach 50% of your net worth (after exemptions). Furthermore, banks may call in loans and credit lines that you personally guaranteed after you are gone, causing cash flow strain or business liquidation.

9. **The second (or third or fourth) generation is not up to the task.** Most family businesses do not survive the next generation of family ownership. Many reasons contribute to this failure, including taxes, inadequate training of successors, and lack of trust and communication among siblings. Is your family business immune? Is the next generation ready? Have you taken the time to fully prepare them to succeed?

10. **Opportunity knocks.** Certain industries are enjoying unprecedented growth and receive very high valuations. Is now the time to take advantage of this prosperity to reduce risk, create a liquidity event, and take some or all of your chips off the table and diversify your assets?

Early planning is vital. The key to all of this is understanding your exit options and choosing the right "one way out" for you, your business, and your family before the time comes. This book is designed to illuminate your options so that you will have your very best opportunity at achieving a smooth, successful exit.

PART ONE
Sales to Outsiders

Chapter 1

A Dream Team Achieves Triple Estimated Valuation

"We have Michael Jordan on our team, so who is your guy? You only have one shot to do this right." That's what our Lincoln Financial Advisors partner Bruce Charleton told a client who had received an unsolicited offer from his biggest customer to buy his company. Feeling pressured and anxious to make a deal, his client came close to making the worst mistake of his financial life. Fortunately, his advisory team saved him and helped him realize triple his estimated value of his company. How did he make it all the way to the promised land? Here's the story...

Objectives
- Evaluate and act on unsolicited purchase offer from biggest customer.
- Value company, and shepherd sale process to best conclusion.

Challenges
- Purchase offer from customer took the owner by surprise.
- Owner needed to identify the best team to evaluate offer and manage the sale.
- M&A team needed to guide the owner and his ability to manage the unknowns around selling his business.
- The buyer was backed by a foreign investor, adding complexity.

The ESG Team

- Dan Prisciotta, CFP®, CPA*, PFS, ChFC®, CBEC®, Managing Partner, Equity Strategies Group (ESG)
- Bruce Charleton, MBA, CLTC®, CBEC®, BII Specialist, The Resource Group
- Kevin, Preferred ESG Investment Banker

Dan: Bruce, how did you get started with this business owner?

Bruce: My relationship with Dennis started in 2008 with me handling his life and disability insurance needs and managing about $100,000 of his investments. Shortly thereafter, he left his corporate job and started a technology business. We would meet several times per year and talk about strategic growth ideas. His company grew rapidly, and in 2019 I brought in Sagemark Consulting Private Wealth Services advisor Tim Veazey to work with me to develop a comprehensive business and estate plan. Our planning department software put an estimated value of $4.5 million on the business at that time. The plan was for Dennis to work another five to 10 years before selling the company, since he was only 47 at the time. Fortunately for him, it didn't work out quite that way.

Dan: What changed?

Bruce: One day Dennis received a letter of intent (LOI) from one of his biggest customers, offering to purchase his business for $10 million. He had to take it seriously because he did not want to endanger the relationship. However, it caught him off guard, and he did not know what to do next. The interested party was pressuring him to enter into a 60-day exclusivity period for the sale. Someone on his board recommended a local business consultant/broker who offered to help him complete the deal for a low fee of $60,000. After doing some background checking on the broker, I was underwhelmed. Referring to the world-class skills of our own advisors and investment banking partners, I told Dennis, "For you right now, it's the 1990s and the NBA championship is on the line. We have Michael Jordan on our team. Who is your guy? You only have one shot to do this right. Do you want to look back with regret that you didn't assemble the best team possible?" Dennis was as tight with money as bark on a tree, so I knew he would regret settling for anything less than maximum value for his business.

Dan: I can certainly appreciate that! This is when you reached out to ESG for help in evaluating the offer. When we attended our initial meeting with Dennis and met his attorneys, we determined that they might be good

> "For you right now, it's the 1990s and the NBA championship is on the line. We have Michael Jordan on our team. Who is your guy?"

at papering transactions but would not be sharp negotiators—that's the job of an investment banker. We also found that the LOI was written very sloppily and clearly favored the buyer. It was nonbinding, and it was highly doubtful whether the buyer would follow through, with every incentive to chew down the price. As we prepared ESG's complimentary MARKETABILITY ASSESSMENT, and thorough review of the financial statements, we also learned that the business's profits had grown from $250,000 in 2017 to $450,000 in 2018 and were approaching $1 million in 2019. After evaluating every aspect of Dennis's business, we brought in our most qualified investment banker for this engagement, Kevin, to represent Dennis in this negotiated sale with the buyer. CCP took on the assignment at a very reasonable flat fee. How would you describe your role after that point, Bruce?

The ESG MARKETABILITY ASSESSMENT

As you embark on the path to sell your business to an outside party, you need ESG's complimentary MARKETABILITY ASSESSMENT. This provides a critical foundation for you and your advisors to determine whether you and your business are ready to sell and what the potential range of values might be, and to evaluate possible mergers and acquisitions (M&A) and investment banking partners who could help you execute your exit. It is the first critical step you will take to learn how to maximize the value of your business.

A MARKETABILITY ASSESSMENT is forward looking and endeavors to estimate what an actual buyer would pay for your company based on a combination of past, current, and future performance. It utilizes various databases to examine prevailing earnings before income, taxes, depreciation, and amortization (EBITDA) multiples and other valuation methods applicable to your business and industry. It also studies comparable sales of similar companies by researching recent similar transactions, where data is available.

A well-prepared MARKETABILITY ASSESSMENT will bring clarity in the following areas:

* An understanding of the value of your business if you were to sell it to a qualified buyer today. A tight range of values is calculated using capitalization of earnings, discounted cash flow, and other methods. (Note that this differs from a historical appraisal prepared for gift or estate tax purposes based on Revenue Ruling 59-60 and similar methods. Those appraisals look backward.)
* Recommendations to enhance value based on an assessment of your company's value drivers and potential value detractors.
* An overview of the current M&A environment and appetite for potential buyers of your business.
* Information regarding the length of time necessary to consummate a sale, and explanation of the steps involved.
* An understanding of the fees earned by M&A firms and investment bankers to help you achieve your exit goals.

The MARKETABILITY ASSESSMENT process also helps select the best-fit M&A or investment banking firm to represent you and your business, based on the criteria described earlier and specific factors, such as its industry expertise, its track record of closing transactions, a proper match of transaction size and type, consideration of the chemistry of the players involved, as well as geographic considerations, such as the company's local, national, and international reach. After gaining this clarity, you then can choose the best-fit firm to represent you and take your company to the marketplace.

Bruce: As an advisor I saw my role as managing my client's emotions and expectations. I knew this process would be complicated and that there would be ups and downs. However, working with you gave me confidence in the process so I was able to keep Dennis calm and explain how the whole thing works, that the buyer's urgency to close did not match his, and that he would be best served if he was patient.

Dan: Kevin, what were the major challenges you faced during this transaction?

Kevin: Just like Bruce, I felt we needed to manage Dennis's inexperience and drive to get this deal done, as we did not want him to send the wrong signals to the buyer. As much as we wanted to approach other potential buyers, Dennis was convinced that this one was a perfect fit! Of course, we hinted that if the buyer did not speed up the process, we would get other offers. Dennis did a tremendous job building his business over many years; however, as he had never been through this sale process before, he was not aware that buyers would request sensitive information, and he was taken back. When the buyer wanted to confirm certain financial data, Dennis became offended because he did not understand the process. He had assumed that the buyer was going to blindly write a large check without any due diligence or negotiation! His impulses could have killed the deal several times if we had not been there to help. Another challenge that caused delay was the need for his next largest customer to sign a contract to continue with the company in order to give the buyer comfort. This turned out to be another waiting game, and Dennis became insistent that we force the buyer to close without it! We explained that you cannot force someone to buy when they are waiting for a piece of critical data such as this.

What *Not* to Do When Someone Offers to Buy Your Company

Have you ever been approached by someone who wants to buy your business? It can be flattering, but if you reveal too much to your suitor, you will end up regretting that you ever met. You're a smart businessperson, but this may be your first time at this game. Here are four key mistakes to avoid:

Mistake 1: Looking Too Eager

You may be burnt out, and the idea of selling your business may feel like the perfect solution to your fatigue, but the last thing you want to do is appear desperate. Instead, politely thank your suitor for their interest. Let them know that your business is not for sale, but you're always open to a strategic discussion. Then call your financial advisor and pull together your business transition / exit planning team.

Mistake 2: Giving Away Your Secrets

Before entering into any discussions, have your suitor execute a confidentiality agreement. Your team will direct you to an M&A attorney who will be able to provide you with one. If you decide to take a meeting, you must play it right. Reiterate that you're not for sale but open to a discussion. Also, meet off-site, not at your office. Let your suitor do 95% of the talking. This will be the opposite of what *they* want, so it requires some thoughtful preparation. Prepare a list of questions that you would like to ask them, such as what kind of customers they target; what their goals are for the future; why they are interested in your company; what barriers they will have to overcome to achieve their aspirations; what they think about their company's valuation. Your suitor may try to take control of the conversation. If that happens, quickly move back to *your* questions. Controlling the conversation allows you to gather some important competitive intelligence and will demonstrate that you are a sophisticated owner unlikely to be blinded by flattery.

Mistake 3: Giving Them a Number

At some point during your conversations, your would-be buyer will try to get a sense of the price at which you would be willing to sell your business. Do not answer this question! Reiterate that you're not for sale, but you're always open to considering expressions of interest. Savvy buyers may be reluctant to take no for an answer and may ask the question a second time with something like, "Sure, but you must have a range you would consider?" Again decline to comment and let them know you'll take any expression of interest they want to prepare seriously. The only thing answering this question will do is put a ceiling on the value of your business. There is no upside to answering it, so defer and let them make the first move.

Mistake 4: Signing a Proprietary Deal

If you receive a written expression of interest, it's time to hire an intermediary to represent you (an M&A advisor or investment banker). Selling your business is not a DIY project. Your suitor will want you to agree to an LOI, which will likely include a "no-shop" clause that eliminates your ability to find a competitive offer. It is called a proprietary deal, and buyers love them because they end up driving down the price and tilt terms in their favor without competition. Your advisory team will likely counsel you against signing an LOI until they complete their process of conducting a competitive auction to attract additional buyers to bid up the price and improve the terms of your deal. If you and your team become convinced that they are truly your best buyer, then your investment banker will conduct a negotiated sale with that buyer to make sure it closes in a timely manner at the best possible price and terms for you.

Dan: How did you finally push this to closure?

Kevin: We remained focused and patient, secured the signed customer contract, and finished our negotiation. But then another problem arose: The buyer was backed by a foreign investor, which meant that the U.S. Department of Justice had to approve the purchase! This added another two months to the process, but we ultimately got that approval and *closed for $15 million—triple the original valuation!* We also significantly improved the terms and conditions, and structured the deal as a stock sale to save taxes. *We managed to get over 14 times current-year*

EBITDA! If we had not been involved, I am confident that this company would have sold for significantly less and cost Dennis much more in taxes, or not closed at all.

"We managed to get over 14 times current-year EBITDA!"

Dan: That's an amazing outcome, especially during a pandemic and without doing a competitive auction. Bruce, how did Dennis feel when it was all over?

Bruce: He was exhausted and happy! He actually said to me, "Bruce, I can't thank you enough for helping me close the sale. I couldn't have gotten it done without your leadership and your team." Of the $15 million he received, Dennis decided to roll over 10% into the new company. Since he is a young man and wants to continue to work, they made him the VP of an entire division, so he still feels like an owner and is able to enjoy the fulfilment that stems from the business. Now, instead of managing a company with 14 employees, he's part of a 200-employee organization with 50 salespeople reporting directly to him. He is in his glory! I told him he now has a first-class problem: He needs a plan to manage his new wealth. So, he again retained Tim and me to develop a plan for his next stage in life. We updated his estate and asset protection plan, and I developed and performed several cash flow models to show that he has achieved financial independence.

Dan: I'm sure managing his investments is part of the new plan.

Bruce: Well, that part became very interesting. A local newspaper issued a press release that publicized the sale after it closed, with Dennis' approval. Every investment firm in town came out of the woodwork and called on Dennis. Initially he wanted to invest one-third with us and one-third with another broker, and play with the remaining third himself. When I walked him through our investment plan, he remarked that I was the only advisor who showed him that he could possibly lose money in the market. Everyone else had presented only the positives. As he put it, "You were the only firm to educate me on this and not just try to sell me." Our honesty came through, so Dennis agreed to place *all* of his investments with us, which will provide him with financial security, and just kept a small portion for himself as "play money." Remember, Dennis also rolled over $1.5 million of equity into the new company, which is exploding in value and should be sold in the near future and provide another major payday.

Dan: Bruce, after this experience with ESG, what are your takeaways?

Bruce: The process could not have gone any better than it did. I'm thrilled about assembling Dennis's team to make a once-in-a-lifetime deal. I personally learned a lot from you and Kevin about focusing on what we can control versus what we can't, and how to sit on my clients' side of the table. I was able to keep Dennis focused on running his business throughout the sales process, which I know resulted in him getting top dollar. And, I didn't have to get into the weeds… I turned that responsibility over to ESG and your preferred investment banking group to get the job done. Overall, this opportunity was a slam-dunk! It paid off big time for Dennis, thanks to the dream team we assembled.

Key Takeaways

- If you receive an unsolicited offer, don't try to sell on your own! You need a hall-of-fame-quality investment banker and dream team.
- Believe in the process, work with the most knowledgeable M&A advisors to determine your optimal valuation, conduct due diligence, and negotiate skillfully. Be patient.
- If you don't want to retire, find the right buyer who can accommodate your desired next chapter in life.

Chapter 2

Patience Turns $15 Million Valuation into $30 Million Sale

*Lincoln Financial Services advisors Rhett Sinclair and Jim
Barnett of Creative Financial Strategies, based in Columbia, South
Carolina, reached out to me regarding a business owner client.
The owner's initial game plan was to work another four to five
years, grow the business, and then sell it for $14–15 million. ESG
performed our complimentary MARKETABILITY ASSESSMENT and
determined that his company was not yet ready to go to market, so
we agreed to put this case on hold for one year and then revisit.
That turned out to be a very wise move, ultimately resulting
in a $30 million business sale!*

Objectives
* Create a liquidity event to get out of managing the company, protect downside risk for the owner, and diversify into liquid assets.
* Remove financial risk. Owner was responsible for all the debt and had signed personal guarantees.
* Leverage the strategic and financial resources of a larger entity.

Challenges
* Needed to trim expenses to improve the bottom line.
* Too many employees hired too quickly.
* Recent earnings had decreased dramatically.

- A KPMG Quality of Earnings (Q of E) report requested by the buyer did not support the original profitability numbers.
- As a result, the original letter of intent of $23.5 million decreased to $12.5 million.

The ESG Team

- Dan Prisciotta, CFP®, CPA*, PFS, ChFC®, CBEC®, Managing Partner, Equity Strategies Group (ESG)
- Jim Barnett, CBEC®, ChFC, CLU, BII Specialist, Creative Financial Strategies/ Lincoln Financial Services
- Rhett Sinclair, CFP®, CLU, Creative Financial Strategies/Lincoln Financial Services
- Mark, Preferred ESG Investment Banker

This business owner, Bill, who was in his mid-40s and married with children, was in the IT services business with a company he founded in 1999. It had multiple locations across two states, employing more than 50 people, and had been recognized in *Inc.* magazine's "5,000 Fastest-Growing Private Companies" list.

Dan: Rhett, what was your background with Bill, and what got him thinking about a sale?

Rhett: We had a great 20-year relationship. I originally set up Bill's company's 401(k) plan and assisted him with key person and buy-sell agreement-funding insurance. His business had been very successful, but all of his wealth was locked up in it. Back in 2018 he was at the point in his life and career where he wanted to do something about that and start enjoying more of the fruits of his labor. He was tired of managing his company and desired liquidity. Since we had built such a trusting and successful relationship, he turned to me. Initially said he wanted to work four to five more years—and even then he wasn't sure if he was emotionally and financially ready to go. At the same time he was aware of a lot of M&A activity in his industry and abundant capital available, and he was getting lots of calls and interest. We needed your expertise to help him understand his exit options, make the best decision for him, and work through the M&A process.

Jim: The owner realized he needed a team of professionals to guide him, so we began by contacting you at ESG. Your complimentary MARKETABILITY ASSESSMENT determined that his company needed to trim expenses and build the bottom line or EBITDA [earnings before interest, taxes, depreciation, and amortization], so we decided to delay the sale for 18 to 24 months while those issues were addressed.

Dan: Pausing the process like that takes real discipline, but it certainly did pay off!

Rhett: Absolutely! The break helped the owner get expenses and the bottom line in much better shape. Then, you conducted a *second* MARKETABILITY ASSESSMENT, which indicated that we finally were ready to market the company for optimal value.

Dan: Mark, at that point we introduced you and your investment banking firm to represent Bill. I understand that after you initially were engaged to move that sale forward, it turned into a much different arrangement. How did the deal evolve?

Mark: Bill wanted us to approach only three potential buyers, *without a deal book*, to achieve his value goal of $14–15 million. The problem was those three companies had no incentive to move quickly and then only offered $8–9 million…that's it! This is not how our typical process works. The whole ordeal felt like death by a thousand paper cuts.

Dan: Not an ideal situation, to say the least. How did you deal with the owner's concerns?

Mark: After we strategized further with Bill, we convinced him to move forward with a full competitive auction process and go to market. *We contacted over 1,000 prospective buyers—800 private equity groups plus 200 strategic buyers. The result was we received 49 signed NDAs [non-disclosure agreements and requests for additional information], and we sent deal books to all of those candidates.* This effort yielded 12 letters of intent [LOI]. We evaluated each LOI carefully to identify those that were the most meaningful, which turned out to be three private equity groups [PEGs]. We looked at which of those were of the highest quality and had funds ready to invest. We then negotiated with each one until we selected the most qualified to sign a formal LOI.

Dan: Why did you and your owner choose that particular PEG as your ultimate buyer?

Mark: This PEG already owned a portfolio company that was in the same industry as our owner's company. Their goal was to add on a complimentary company and grow both aggressively. We did our due diligence on this PEG and found them to be a perfect match.

> "We contacted over 1,000 prospective buyers—800 private equity groups plus 200 strategic buyers. The result was we received 49 signed NDAs, and we sent deal books to all of those candidates."

Dan: Mark, what were some of the other challenges that you encountered during this transaction?

Mark: This was a very complicated deal. There were tons of add-backs to EBITDA, some of which were obvious, while others were a difficult sell to the PEG. The client had hired too many people, the wrong leadership team was in the C-suite, and we were trying to justify these investments. The first step in due diligence was that the PEG buyer wanted a Q of E [quality of earnings] performed by KPMG. This process became extremely complicated and protracted. Throughout 2018, our client's earnings had gone down dramatically, and the Q of E did not support the original numbers—not even close! The company was losing money every month, and it was like catching a falling knife. The original LOI of $23.5 million decreased to $12.5 million. At that point I told the PEG that this is not going to work. I then proceeded to negotiate further for a higher price and more favorable tax treatment for our seller. Our goal was to sell the stock in his company, not his assets.

Why Use an Investment Banker?

There are many reasons to use an investment banker for selling your business. This is not a do-it-yourself event. You only get one chance to do it right—no mulligans!

- **Finding buyers:** Investment bankers supplement your knowledge of your markets and potential partners by tapping into their professional contacts and networks, investor databases, and expertise to identify and connect with interested, qualified buyers.
- **Negotiating the deal:** Investment bankers take the lead in negotiating the deal terms—not only the purchase price but also the terms and conditions, timing, process, and other major considerations of the transaction, including achievement of favorable tax savings for the seller.
- **Managing the sales process:** Investment bankers are often quarterbacks for the entire transaction process. They are the ones who are responsible for keeping the transaction process competitive, coordinating between all of the different aspects of the transaction, managing a broad team of other advisors, and keeping the transaction moving to a closing in a timely manner.
- **Adding to your credibility as the seller:** Engaging a quality investment bank illustrates to all of the parties involved that there is a genuine commitment to exploring the transaction and that there is professional representation, thus increasing the likelihood of a successful closing.
- **Preparing your company for sale:** Sellers are rarely prepared for the intense scrutiny they will be subject to by experienced buyers and their litany of professional transaction advisors. Investment bankers can help you with this preparation, which can involve everything from preparing detailed financial models and projections to in-depth customer analyses to working with management to prepare them for an intense transaction process.

- **Educating and coaching services:** The vast majority of business owners have never closed a transaction. Quality investment bankers have managed hundreds of transactions and can bring the benefits of that experience to the owner.
- **Structuring the transaction:** Transactions can involve various forms of consideration, such as cash, equity, seller notes, earnouts, and other forms of contingent consideration. Investment bankers can structure each transaction specifically to address the needs and desires of both sellers and buyers, thus providing creative solutions for potentially conflicting transaction objectives.
- **Enabling owners to run the business:** The transaction process is an intensive process for sellers to endure, especially as they are trying to run the day- to-day operations of their company. By taking on most of the day-to-day work, investment bankers enable business owners to focus on growing their business rather than managing the transaction process, which typically lasts for between six and nine months.

Dan: What did your negotiations yield?

Mark: We wound up closing the transaction in March 2019 with an astounding result. The cash portion up front was $14,260,000 plus a $6 million earnout over two years (half cash; half additional equity). We negotiated a stock deal rather than an asset deal, which was a major win. In addition, the rollover equity is not currently taxed and was structured in a way so that the owner received a nondiluted interest in the larger entity at closing, which gave him significantly more equity! Also, $2.4 million was rolled over tax-free into the PEG. The expectation was that when the combined companies are sold in three to five years, he could earn at least three to four times his investment, or another $10 million plus! In addition, the PEG paid for about $250,000 of closing-related benefits (which they normally do not pay), and our happy client will continue to work for several years as VP of business development, receiving a generous salary and perks. He also has a seat on the board of the new company. *All in, he receives over $30 million of value!*

> **Pro Tip:** We have seen many instances where owners (and investment bankers who should have known better) rushed to market prematurely. The consequences were severe. Buyers kicked the tires but did not make serious offers, and the prices they considered paying were insulting. Often, they wasted money and emotion, and it took years to recover and consider a proper exit. Objectivity and patience are key elements. Ask yourself: Is moving toward a sale at this time in your best interest?

Dan: Mark, that is an incredible result, especially after all of the challenges that came up during the due diligence process and the horrendous year the business suffered through! How did you keep the owner on track?

Mark: Jim, Rhett, and I continually reminded Bill of his three main objectives, and that the offer we negotiated exceeded his expectations. During the most challenging portions of the process, I acted as both an expert and trusted counselor. I spoke with him on a regular basis and talked him off the ledge several times.

Dan: Jim and Rhett, how did Bill feel when the deal closed?

Rhett: He was excited and relieved at the same time that the process was over and that the deal happened. Selling was an incredibly emotional experience for him, almost traumatic. A lot of psychology and counseling was needed to get him comfortable with his decision.

Dan: Jim, a lot of tax planning went into this case as well, didn't it?

Jim: Yes, ESG's investment banking firm *negotiated a stock sale rather than an asset sale,* which was a major win. In addition, the *rollover equity is not currently taxed* and was structured it in a way that *he received a nondiluted interest in the larger entity at closing,* which gave him significantly more equity. Finally, we designed a tax strategy with 20% of the business going into a NIMCRUT [net income with makeup charitable remainder unitrust], which saved even more taxes! *Bill received an income tax deduction for the value of the stock contributed to the trust.* He will receive income for the rest of his life, and the assets in the trust are excluded from estate taxes. In addition, Bill's favorite charities will benefit from the trust proceeds when he is gone.

Dan: Fantastic job!! Are you and Rhett helping Bill invest the proceeds?

Rhett: Yes, and he has become very risk-averse. Therefore, we designed a portfolio that provides downside protection, liquidity, and some appreciation potential. He is also interested in deferring income taxes. In addition, we are introducing concepts to protect and transfer wealth efficiently to his family.

Jim: Furthermore, our experience with ESG was everything we expected and more. Dan, you expertly handled the initial meetings with our owner, gathered all of the necessary data, and did not one but two Marketability Assessments. You set the stage for the process our owner would go through to sell his business. Mark was an excellent choice and is one of the sharpest professionals I've ever worked with in my 31-year career!

Dan: Thanks, guys. You were a pleasure to work with, and Mark and I appreciate the opportunity to serve you and your client to help achieve his lifetime liquidity event!

Key Takeaways

- Be patient and learn from the Marketability Assessment.
- Take whatever time is needed to prepare your business to maximize its value.
- Engage a professional team of experts to provide honest feedback about value and timing.
- Effectively use ESG to successfully set the stage for the sales process, gather all of the necessary data, conduct a Marketability Assessment (or two), and choose the best-fit investment bank to lead negotiations.
- Tax planning is key. It's not just the selling price that is important; it's what you walk away with after taxes that really counts.

Chapter 3

From Pandemic Challenge To Savory Exit

You've heard it before: Timing is everything. It may be a cliché, but it's usually the truth, and in this case, it paid off big time. Peter and Sam, ages 54 and 69, decided they were ready to sell their thriving craft cheese businesses while retaining a one-third ownership in a related company with a majority partner. However, although they had a desire to exit, they did not have a strategy, and they soon were to also face the challenge of a worldwide pandemic during which market opportunities slowed dramatically. Fortunately, they connected with ESG, which resulted in a coordinated, well-timed transaction that netted them twice their initial valuation expectation.

Objectives
- Sell craft cheese business while retaining one-third ownership in a related company.
- Achieve maximum value for the company.
- Invest proceeds in the optimal post-sale outcome.

Challenges
- Owners desired an exit but didn't have a strategy.
- Worldwide pandemic interrupted sale
- Employees were stretched thin.
- Company was regular C corporation, potentially subject to double taxation upon sale.

The ESG Team

- Dan Prisciotta, CFP®, CPA*, PFS, ChFC®, CBEC®, Managing Partner, Equity Strategies Group (ESG)
- Kevin, Preferred ESG Investment Banker

Dan: Kevin, as you know, ESG first got involved with planning Peter and Sam's exit planning at the beginning of 2017. They had found great success offering acclaimed cheeses that were 100% natural and produced through a unique way of smoking and flavoring, including vegetarian and kosher varieties. They had decided that they could not continue running the business much longer because they were increasingly feeling stressed out. Their 10 employees were stretched thin and overworked, and so were they!

Kevin: You shared with me later that in 2017 they did not have any succession management—they lacked the technology and salespeople, and at that stage in their careers they did not want to take on significant debt to grow, sign personal guarantees, or assume additional risk...and that they simply were not emotionally ready to sell at that time. So what did you do then?

Dan: You are correct, Kevin. Of course, we stayed in touch, and by the end of 2019 they observed that many of their friends in the industry were selling their businesses and taking advantage of the frothy M&A market. They would listen whenever a prospective buyer expressed interest. I explained to them that the right buyer rarely just comes along, so they needed a strategy. To consummate a transaction and maximize value they would need to engage in a process to actively market and sell the company...and of course we discussed that in detail!

We gathered the information necessary to prepare our complimentary Marketability Assessment and demonstrate our capabilities. We explored a wide range of options—for example, a 100% sale or partial sale, or whether to sell companies separately or together—and determined a possible valuation range. Their accounting firm also made a proposal for handling the sale, but we wisely encouraged them to seek a second opinion and interview another M&A firm.

Kevin: And that's when I entered the picture...

Dan: Right! At that point we brought you into the discussions as a food industry M&A expert. Peter and Sam were very impressed and retained your firm to represent their company.

Kevin: We were happy to be on board. The owners were quite pleased with our initial $14–15 million valuation determined by your MARKET-ABILITY ASSESSMENT. We created our buyer list and book, and went to market. Almost immediately we received 77 responses and 41 signed NDAs! We actually received several written letters of intent [LOI] and were getting ready for several management visits during the first week of March 2020. You know what happened then.

Dan: Of course, it was the onset of the pandemic. The world stopped. How did you deal with this?

Kevin: We proposed to Peter and Sam that we put the engagement on pause until things opened up a bit. We suspended our monthly retainer fees for six months, which was appreciated and further solidified our relationship. At that point they truly understood that we had their best interest at heart, though we continued to market the business throughout this time frame. And...our strategy paid off! During the downtime, Peter and Sam developed several new products, and all those people staying home for months actually consumed more cheese than ever before. EBITDA [earnings before interest, taxes, depreciation and amortization] rose from less than $3 million to almost $4 million!

Dan: Was that the combined EBITDA of both cheese companies?

Kevin: Yes, and then we uncovered the fact that they owned a small interest in a startup internet-based cheese company that was on track to earn about $200,000 in net income. That company had only been around for eight months!

Finding the Right Investment Banker for You

Choosing the right transaction intermediary to help you sell your company, whether that is an investment banker or M&A advisor, is both a subjective and an objective decision. As with any industry, you will find both high quality firms and those that are inferior. One of ESG's value propositions is helping business owners choose the best-fit investment banker to help them execute their desired exit path. We have spent almost twenty years selecting what we believe to be the premiere network of investment bankers and M&A firms in the country. Because our business owner clients are in virtually every industry and location, we have built a diverse platform and rigorously vetted and researched our approved alliance partners prior to introducing them to our valued clients. It is critical that you and your trusted advisors carefully select the right firm to execute your transaction and help lead you on the journey of selling your business. Does the firm you are considering have knowledge of and experience in buying and selling businesses in your industry? Is it the right sized firm for your transaction (not too large or small)? Will you receive senior-level attention? Does your investment banker have any conflicts of interest? What is their track record of success? Is the firm well-staffed and well supported? You need to "click" with your investment banker, because together you will be making some of the most critical decisions of your life. It is important that you trust each other.

Objectively, you want someone who understands you and your industry and has deep and current experience selling entrepreneur-owned middle-market companies like yours.

In addition to probing their experience, you need to assess your transaction intermediaries' people skills. Specifically, carefully consider whether they possess these qualities:
- Strong interpersonal communications skills.
- A deep understanding of what motivates people.
- The ability to predict behavior and adapt to different people, situations, and levels of intensity.

- Superior sales skills.
- The ability to tell the story of your company in a compelling way.
- Interest in your company's competitive advantages. Do they have ideas about how to leverage it?
- The skills to formulate creative marketing strategies.
- Sensitivity to your need for confidentiality and commitment to protecting it.
- Good listening skills.
- The ability to provide examples of how they have anticipated (and dealt with) challenges in the past.

One quality that is a little more difficult to assess is the investment banker's ability to separate unimportant issues from deal breakers, and to distinguish between a bluff and a deal-ending condition. You also want someone who can separate serious from halfhearted buyers. If your candidate cannot accurately make these judgment calls, it is likely that deal momentum will suffer and your deal will collapse before closing. You want an experienced guide with a superior process to obtain the premium results you deserve.

Dan: So, did buyers have interest in purchasing all three companies?

Kevin: Once we packaged them correctly, they absolutely did! We wound up selling the two main companies plus the related business real estate for $28 million. We then sold the startup for ten times EBITDA, for a total transaction value of $30.3 million!

Dan: Outstanding results! I know that the process became intense toward the end, as it often does.

Kevin: It did, Dan. You could say we had a challenging time helping Peter and Sam remain calm during the negotiations, as they were inexperienced and could have potentially derailed the most favorable outcome. The due diligence process was wearing them out. But our guidance, patience, and perseverance certainly paid off.

"I negotiated it up to $28 million, plus over $2 million for the third company, for a total selling price of $30.3 million!"

Dan: Who was the ultimate buyer, and can you take us through how you closed the deal?

Kevin: We sourced a large private equity group that was on a new mission to roll up and consolidate the cheese industry. The PEG owned 12 other companies, but this was their first acquisition in the cheese business. They recognize that cheese is now considered healthy and is a highly desirable industry. When we initially contacted them, they were so eager that they wanted to preempt any other buyers and asked us to take it off the market immediately. They asked how much it would take to take it off the market and get a deal done. *I told them $31 million, without the internet-based cheese company. They countered with $26 million, and I negotiated it up to $28 million, plus over $2 million for the third company, for a total selling price of $30.3 million!*

Dan: Since you more than doubled Peter and Sam's initial value expectation, they were very pleased indeed. Now Peter is looking forward to a happy, financially independent retirement. Sam, who is much younger, will continue to stay on and run the company for the new owner under a lucrative employment agreement. Clearly, their delicious craft cheeses helped us all produce a very savory deal!

Key Takeaways

- Don't jump at the first offer; explore a range of exit options to find the one best for you.
- Work with ESG to identify the best M&A advisor for your industry.
- If you have an unexpected pause, be patient and use the time to increase the value of your company.
- Rely on your exit planning team during valuation, marketing and negotiations.

Chapter 4

Owner Expected $22–25 Million; ESG Result: $31.5 Million in Cash

"Exit planning is the most important thing you can do for me!" This is a direct quote from a 64-year-old business owner to Chartered Financial Consultant and Certified Business Exit Consultant Tim Donovan. Tim and ESG ultimately helped the owner sell his business for $31.5 million in an all-cash transaction in July 2020. What's amazing is the initial value range expectation during our MARKETABILITY ASSESSMENT was only $22–25 million. How did we achieve this phenomenal result for this owner, especially during the COVID-19 pandemic?

Objectives
+ Conduct ESG's MARKETABILITY ASSESSMENT to understand the company's value.
+ Sell inherited metals business for the best price to a select buyer.
+ Connect with the best team of experts to guide the M&A process.
+ Enjoy retirement cash flow and create optimal wealth preservation for owner's family.

Challenges
+ Owner initially had no exit plan, even though he thought and worried about it often.
+ Family succession was not possible, and his management team lacked the cash, creditworthiness, and risk tolerance to purchase the business from him.

- Owner was very particular about the type of buyer who would be acceptable.
- Potential buyers were concerned about sustainability of earnings.
- EBITDA plummeted almost 40% during due diligence time frame.
- COVID-19 pandemic caused the buyer's original financing bank to pull out.

The ESG Team

- Dan Prisciotta, CFP®, CPA*, PFS, ChFC®, CBEC®, Managing Partner, Equity Strategies Group (ESG)
- Tim Donovan, ChFC, CBEC, BII Specialist, Family Wealth Management Group, LLC
- Nick and Chris, Preferred ESG Investment Bankers

Dan: Congratulations, Tim. How did you get started with this business owner?

Tim: I connected with George through a strong client referral about five years ago. During our initial discussion, I described the four areas of financial planning that we do, including business succession. At that point he stopped me and said, "I don't have a plan for that! If you can help, that is the most important thing you can do for me!" George acknowledged that his 60% ownership stake was by far his biggest asset. The business was started in 1950 by his grandfather, who gave stock to his son (George's father) and to multiple family members and employees in lieu of cash wages. George later gave 5% to his CFO.

Dan: What succession strategies had George tried previously?

Tim: After ruling out family succession, he looked at his management team. As is often the case, they had the desire but lacked the cash, creditworthiness, and risk tolerance to buy him out. He even entered into discussions to sell to one of his customers, which did not come to fruition. George initially met with several local investment bankers before he connected with me but was undecided on that approach. When I described our process at Lincoln, including ESG and your access to 20 premier investment banking partners, he was eager for a conversation with you and the development of your complimentary MARKETABILITY ASSESSMENT.

7 Steps to a Successful Exit

Step 1: Exit objectives. Determine your planning objectives with respect to exiting your business, such as:
- What is your desired departure date? Now? One year from now? Ten years or more?
- How much income do you need to achieve financial security (your "value gap" expressed as a lump sum or annual income need/ shortage)?
- What type of purchaser would be ideal for you—a family member, internal employees or managers, another buyer in your industry, or a financial buyer, such as a private equity group?

Step 2: Valuation. Do you really know how much your business is worth in today's economy?

Step 3: Making the business more valuable. Do you know how to effectively increase the value of your ownership interest prior to exit?

Step 4: Sale to a third party. Do you know how to sell your business to a third party (if that is your goal) in a way that will maximize your cash and minimize your tax liability?

Step 5: Transfer to co-owners or family. Do you know how to transfer your business to family members, co-owners, or employees and pay the least possible amount in taxes, while enjoying maximum financial security?

Step 6: Contingency planning. Have you implemented all necessary steps and up-to-date documents to ensure that the business continues even if you don't?

Step 7: Wealth preservation planning. Have you provided for your family's security should you die or become incapacitated? Have you planned for the distribution of your business and other assets, while minimizing exposure to the 40% federal estate tax? A will or trust is not enough. Business owners need advanced-level wealth preservation planning to address their special assets and circumstances and avoid forced liquidation of their business and real estate for pennies on the dollar.

Dan: During the construction of our MARKETABILITY ASSESSMENT, we reached out to Nick, the managing director of his investment banking firm, and his metals industry expert, Chris. Our calculations indicated a value range of $22–25 million, which satisfied George enough to retain our investment banking partners and go to market. Why this investment bank for this particular transaction? They offered industry expertise, a superior scale of platform and resources (as compared to the local investment bankers George had been considering), a dedicated deal team that included two senior-level investment bankers (unusual for a transaction of this size), along with a great personality and values fit. Our team also had the right experience in working with multigenerational family businesses. Nick and Chris, what challenges did you face?

Nick: Dan, the major challenge initially was finding a buyer that George would approve. He placed quite a few restrictions on us. For example, for competitive reasons, he did not want us to approach strategic buyers in his industry. Even though we assured him that we would maintain confidentiality, he declined. Also, he did not want to sell to an international buyer or just any private equity group. Therefore, we had to find a domestic long-term family office–type buyer.

Dan: Can you walk us though that process?

Nick: Sure. We identified 80 candidates that met George's strict criteria, of which 73 signed confidentiality agreements to receive a book. We garnered 10 indications of interest, which led to six management presentations and submission of six LOIs[letters of intent].. Most offers were in the $15–20 million range, and all were concerned about sustainability of earnings. There were other complications as well. Within his metals business, George faced stiff tariffs, environmental issues, and decreasing revenue due to COVID. Originally his trailing twelve months EBITDA was $8 million, but once we found the right buyer and signed a final LOI, EBITDA plummeted almost 40% (vs. 2019) during due diligence! Following that, the commercial bank providing financing pulled out because of the pandemic and left the buyer high and dry. Fortunately, we have excellent relationships in the commercial banking industry and brought in a new lender who closed the loan in less than three weeks. We then closed the sales transaction for $31.5 million with the highest and best buyer for George.

Dan: Amazing job! Who was the buyer, and how did you negotiate such a high selling price?

Chris: Finding the right buyer was the key to this successful sale. We sold to a diversified holding company whose majority shareholder was a family office. They wanted George's business for several reasons: It had a rich history (over 70 years) with dominant market share in specialty niche products. Additionally, the management team was relatively young and very sharp: George's right-hand person, in his 40s, was ready to step into the leadership role with his team right behind him, and a family office making an investment like this really needs shrewd operators to actually run the business. George was a major advocate for his management team and wanted his business to wind up in the right hands. The buyer bought the future vision with George's team in place. The buyer also is bullish on U.S. manufacturing, and this business is a vital link in our nation's supply chain.

Dan: The company is a regular C corporation. How did you minimize income taxes?

Chris: We absolutely needed a stock sale so that George would be taxed at the favorable long-term capital gains rate. We pushed hard and won! In fact, there were multiple minority family shareholders who had no idea they still owned the stock and did not expect any value. Several of them received $500,000 checks. You can imagine their reactions.

Dan: Tim, how did George feel about the entire experience when it was all over?

Tim: George and his CFO raved about our team's professionalism, values, and diligence. They never gave up on this deal despite many setbacks. The difference between our ESG investment bankers and the local firms he initially met with was staggering. Our comprehensive financial planning process culminated in this successful exit. George and his CFO have now become investment and insurance clients of mine. In addition to the sales proceeds, their 401(k) plans will be rolled over to IRAs, which I will manage. Retirement income planning was essential for George and his wife. I am pleased to say that they will have plenty of retirement income. We also updated their estate plan to make certain that their wealth will pass on to their eight children and their 15 (and counting!) grandchildren. George has certainly satisfied his value gap and looks forward in retirement to "going back to school"—spending plenty of time reading and doing things he didn't have time for over his long and illustrious career!

Key Takeaways

- Business owners make excellent clients. There are so many ways to deliver value, including succession and exit planning.
- Evaluate different succession and exit paths (family, management) in decision making.
- Use a major investment banking firm for industry expertise, a superior scale of platform and resources, senior-level attention, values fit, and experience with multigenerational family businesses.
- Minimize income taxes with a stock sale (rather than an asset sale).
- A strong existing management team can serve as a valuable asset in the sale.
- Dig into business valuation—you could be pleasantly surprised!

Chapter 5

Government Contractor Overcomes Client Loss for a Super Sale

Our married owners, Larry and Felice, operated a business dedicated to providing consulting and technical services to government clients, including the U.S. intelligence community, Department of Defense, and other federal agencies. They had grown up very poor, but at age 50 founded their firm with plans to sell it at 60! Great success followed, but the 2008 recession and the loss of two major clients threatened to upend their master plan. Thanks to a top-notch exit team assembled by ESG, including Sagemark Planner Mark Sherno and ESG preferred investment banker Doug, we overcame the challenges and reached their goal—taking good care of their employees and securing their own financial independence.

Objectives
- Exit from business during a period of economic recession.
- Owners wanted out by age 60.
- Enjoy retirement with optimal wealth preservation.

Challenges
- In just one year the business lost two large government contracts and shrunk by 80%.

- First the owners and then the CFO attempted to sell the business themselves without any M&A experience. Results were dismal and potentially damaged the market's view of the business.
- The owners were extremely confidential, almost secretive.

The ESG Team

- Dan Prisciotta, CFP®, CPA*, PFS, ChFC®, CBEC®, Managing Partner, Equity Strategies Group (ESG)
- Mark Sherno, CFP®, ChFC®, CMFC, CBEC®, BII Specialist, The Resource Group
- Doug, Preferred ESG Investment Banker

Dan: Mark, this was a long-term proposition. You initially introduced Larry and Felice to ESG around 2010. However, after delving into their goals and expectations through a series of in-depth discussions, we and the owners agreed that they weren't quite emotionally ready to exit at that time. In addition, they were waiting for tax rates to go down and had inflated valuation expectations that probably could not be satisfied at that time.

Mark: That's exactly right, Dan. Larry and Felice were a bona fide rags-to-riches story—they grew up very poor and really had nothing. They worked for other companies, but never had equity or extra money even though they made the companies they worked for more valuable. Together they started this company at age 50. They built it from scratch. They had no emotional attachment to the business. *They started it for the purpose of selling it.*

Dan: But then trouble hit…

Mark: Yup. Back when we first connected, their business had 600 employees and was worth significantly more than just a year later, when the landscape of their industry changed dramatically. During the interim they had lost two large government contracts and had shrunk to around 100 employees. It all happened very quickly!

Dan: I'll say! What led to this unfortunate and rapid decline?

Mark: There were multiple factors. The recession of 2008 had just happened, and the owners started making some serious mistakes. First, they tried to sell the business on their own—a disaster. Then the CFO offered to help sell the business himself in order to avoid paying fees to investment bankers or merger and acquisition [M&A] specialists. Another disaster! It quickly became pretty obvious that he didn't have a process to identify potential buyers, present the business in the proper light, and then negotiate and close a deal.

Dan: That's a huge mistake that a lot of inexperienced business owners have made—the proverbial penny-wise and pound-foolish approach. Going that route usually turns out poorly. So what did you do then?

Mark: At this point, I advised Larry and Felice to rethink their exit strategy, or lack thereof! Timing became critical. They always had figured that they wanted out before age 60, and guess what? The time had snuck up on them, and they were at that milestone! Thus far, their poor timing with the recession coupled with some inexperienced moves threatened to torpedo their plans. But that was about to change…

Dan: And that's where we came in, again.

Mark: Fortunately, yes! Through ESG's process, anchored by your complimentary MARKETABILITY ASSESSMENT that you delivered at the outset of our work on this, we appropriately valued their company and determined what we had to do to ensure maximum value going forward. Certain expenses were trimmed or deferred, their financial reporting was improved, and some personnel changes were made. At that point we introduced Larry and Felice to one of our preferred investment bankers, Doug, whose firm has expertise in selling government contractors. The owners recognized their value and hired Doug and his team to represent their company.

Maximizing Government Contractor Sales

Government contractors operate in a highly specialized market. As such, there are key considerations to preparing to sell your company and maximize value:

Size matters: Buyers look for government contractors with at least $5 million EBITDA for a platform company. The market of buyers for companies below $2 million EBITDA is significantly smaller.

Quality of revenue: Companies with majority full and open contracts see multiples 1–4 times EBITDA higher relative to companies primarily executing small business set-aside contracts, with 8(a) companies having very limited or no markets. Competing and winning full and open contracts is critical for a government contractor looking to sell.

Maximize EBITDA: There is no substitute for EBITDA. It reflects the value of work performed. Having lots of cost plus fixed-fee contracts with low margin and lots of revenue is suboptimal. More firm-fixed price (FFP) and time and materials (T&M) work with strong history of performance will drive the potential of EBITDA. Don't sacrifice profit for revenue.

Backlog is gold: Having contract backlog that is at least 3 times annual revenue gets buyers attention: It provides a strong foundation for expected cash flows. Also, software as a service that provides long-term, recurring revenue will often be valued as a multiple of revenue, and buyers love this model.

Pipeline is jet fuel: The richness and depth of a weighted pipeline creates an asset that buyers can leverage. A buyer wants to triple their value in a five- to six-year time horizon, and a strong pipeline provides the vehicle to achieve that goal. Building a strong pipeline that is supported by business development activities is vital. You can't just create a list of opportunities; it must be supportable.

Value of services: Firms providing cleared solutions for intelligence agencies are valued much higher than firms doing IT network mainte-nance. There is a strong correlation between the value the work a contractor provides and the value a buyer places on that company. Creating value through software development or engineering design fetches a higher price.

Customer concentration is positive: This is unique in the govern-ment contracting market. In most industries, buyers want work with any one customer to be less than 20% of total revenue. However, in govern-ment contracting, buyers want to see stickiness and depth with customers and like to see revenue concentrated with some big end customers. One exception is they don't want all of the eggs in one basket from a contract standpoint. The best case is multiple task orders and/or multiple existing contracts with big customers.

Strong infrastructure: If you want to exit post-closing, then there better be a strong management team in place. If you incentivize the management team post-closing, this gives the buyer long-term assurance. You are basically selling contracts and people. Keeping the best people in place increases buyer appetite. If you want to stay, it's still beneficial that the team that built success will remain post-closing.

Willingness to stay on: Private equity buyers who are looking for larger-platform companies generally want the sellers to stay on for three years or more and create an incentive structure around that commitment. However, private equity companies that already have a suitable platform company are generally open to a much shorter commitment.

Timing is critical: Valuations of all government contractors are impacted positively or negatively by the federal budget trend in general and the trends in their government agencies and even the trend in certain contracts.

Dan: Doug, your expertise in selling government contractors definitely came in handy on this deal. What challenges did you face in finding the ideal buyer?

Doug: Well, Dan, this was a tight niche.

Dan: What did the process look like?

Doug: We approached 70 potential buyers, which resulted in three solid offers. The entire process took 11 months to close. The chosen offer exceeded Larry and Felice's expectations of $10 million. In addition to the sale price, there was a lot of excess cash on the corporate balance sheet to distribute. They stockpiled cash of $2 million on their corporate balance sheet, which was well in excess of their working capital needs.

We were able to distribute that to Larry and Felice. Eleven months later, their exit goal of $15 million was achieved!

Why Use an M&A Advisor to Sell My Business?

From time to time, the question arises: "Why should I use an M&A firm? Can't I sell my business on my own?" There are a multitude of reasons why you, as a business owner, should not endeavor to sell your own business.

It is natural and understandable to conceive why you might feel that you could and should sell your own business. After all, you know your business inside and out and have an excellent grasp of your industry. However, it does not mean that you will have the time and expertise in someone else's field of endeavor. For that you need a full-time professional M&A advisor or investment banker to find, negotiate, and close the best possible deal to maximize the sales price of your business. An M&A advisor will assist you in these innumerable, exceedingly valuable ways:

- Assess your business's value more accurately.
- Anticipate future challenges in the sales process.
- Develop, validate, and document historical and projected financials.
- Coordinate with other advisors not already on board.
- Identify and evaluate potential types of buyers.
- Develop marketing strategies for your business.
- Identify specific potential buyers.
- Prepare documentation to market your company.
- Initiate contact with potential buyers.
- Obtain signed confidentiality agreements in the marketplace.
- Discretely provide prospective buyers with the detailed information necessary to get top value.
- Obtain indications of interest and arrange for site visits.
- Research and qualify these specific interested buyers.
- Prepare and orchestrate the buyer's visits to your company.
- Create an infrastructure for maintaining momentum.
- Monitor the flow of additional information between seller and buyer.

- Obtain positive indications of value and terms.
- Evaluate alternative proposals.
- Negotiate a term sheet or a letter of intent.
- Prepare your company for due diligence.
- Organize and lead the due diligence process.
- Continually track progress and open issues.
- Help compile the disclosure statement.
- Help compile other closing deliverables.
- Assist negotiating business and financing issues in the definitive agreement.
- Remain on the scene or on duty until the deal ultimately closes.

Selling a business is often the single largest financial transaction in the life of a business owner. There is no second chance to do it over. You have one opportunity to do it right the first and, likely, only time. For details on each of these M&A tasks, visit www.youronewayout.com.

Dan: Any challenges encountered along the way?

Doug: Our owners were extremely confidential, almost secretive. They did not tell their employees of the sale until after closing. However, they ultimately were very generous and did create a retention pool and shared some of their sale proceeds with employees who stayed on with the new owner.

Dan: What feedback did you receive?

Doug: As president of our investment bank, I lead a team. Larry and Felice told me on more than one occasion, "Wow! We really like it when a team of investment bankers work together on our behalf." The team we assembled was very proactive and accessible.

Dan: It was a long and winding road! What lessons can be learned?

Mark: Follow a process. Help your owners stay focused on the goal— they wanted to get out. Keep your eye on the prize! Don't get distracted. They made so much money in a short period of time that they had no value gap or urgency, so they made mistakes. They previously hired the wrong firm, brought in by their CFO, at a low fee and with no industry expertise. Consequently, that firm didn't have a structured process to evaluate and take them to market. The low up-front fee

"Follow a process. Help your owners stay focused on the goal—they wanted to get out. Keep your eye on the prize! Don't get distracted."

was a way to get them engaged and paying a monthly retainer. Nothing really happened after that. Six months had passed, and there was really very little progress. Once that firm's exclusivity period was up, I went to Larry and Felice with urgency and said, "If we don't change course pretty quickly, you're going to have to compromise on getting out at age 60." That's when we got them back on track by reaching out to ESG.

Dan: How satisfied were they with ESG and our preferred investment banker?

Mark: Very satisfied! After going through your process, including your MARKETABILITY ASSESSMENT, they became very comfortable with Doug and his team. Doug is qualified and capable, and he had great people skills and chemistry with our owners. They said, "We had the utmost confidence and respect for Doug because he is an expert in his field. Paying his fee was the best decision we ever made!" They were very pleased with the all-cash deal (no earnout) and six-month transition period.

Dan: What's next for your happy sellers?

Mark: They really haven't had a vacation yet! They plan to spend more time with their children and grandchildren. They want to chill and buy a third boat. Larry is the first one in his family to hit the ball out of the park financially, and I'm really excited for them as they embark on their next adventure.

Dan: Mark, what ongoing investments came as a result of this liquidity event?

Mark: As part of their overall plan, we helped them put $8 million into professionally managed investments. They also wanted to invest in some sophisticated investments, such as collateral loans. They needed

$26,000 per month to achieve financial independence, and that was accomplished easily with the portfolio we designed, including an "over-funded" variable universal life insurance policy that includes cash value, investment variety, flexible premiums, and a flexible death benefit. I continue to manage the company's $6 million defined benefit plan after the sale, while the existing employees stay in place. I also helped Larry and Felice acquire a survivorship universal life policy owned by an irrevocable family dynasty trust for estate planning purposes.

Dan: Gentlemen, that was truly a job well done! Thanks to you and your very capable teams for helping Larry and Felice capture their vision of the American Dream!

Key Takeaways

* Don't try to sell a company on your own! Instead, build a quality, experienced team that understands your industry and includes an investment banking expert.
* Follow a proven, defined process.
* Stay focused on the goal. Keep your eye on the prize! Don't get distracted.
* Rely on your financial advisor to help assure that your retirement, investment, and estate plans are custom-tailored for your family, lifestyle, and goals.

Chapter 6

A "3 for 1" Package Turns a $30 Million Offer into a $55 Million Sale

Susan, the owner of a construction firm, was thinking about selling her business and had received an unsolicited offer of $30 million. However, she had no sales process nor any idea of how much she actually could receive after a proper evaluation. Her financial advisor, Rob Grizzard, introduced her to Equity Strategies Group, which provided a complimentary MARKETABILITY ASSESSMENT to evaluate whether the offer was reasonable. We then established a process and brought the necessary specialists onto the exit team. The ESG result: $55 million! How was this accomplished?

Objectives
- Exit three related businesses as a co-owner and sole owner.
- Evaluate an initial unsolicited offer of $30 million.
- Use proceeds for a dream retirement.

Challenges
- Susan received an offer before she really knew how much her company was worth.
- Susan owned 100% of the company that she initially wanted to sell, 50% of another related company, and 100% of a third company.
- It took months to get clean financial statements suitable for a sale and closing process.

- Buyer tried to lower the price at the 11th hour.

The ESG Team
- Dan Prisciotta, CFP®, CPA*, PFS, ChFC®, CBEC®, Managing Partner, Equity Strategies Group (ESG)
- Rob Grizzard, K&G Financial Services, Nexus Financial
- Emrich Stellar Jr., ChFC, CLU, CBEC, Stellar Advisor, BII Specialist, Mid-Atlantic Regional Partner of ESG
- Doug, April, and Eric, Preferred ESG Investment Bankers

Dan: Rob, tell us how your relationship with this business owner started and evolved over the years.

Rob: Susan became a friend of mine about 10 years ago. Over that period, I would ask about her business and let her know of the services we could bring to the table. One day after asking about her 401(k) plan, she allowed us access to the plan information. My partner, Sam Kouri, and I did our due diligence and reviewed the fee structure and the plan's compliance situation. Long story short, there were issues with the plan that needed to be resolved. Susan saw value in what we brought to the table and asked us to take over the company's 401(k) plan. From that point we became her go-to advisors for retirement planning and insurance needs.

Dan: That's a superb beginning to this story. So, what happened then?

Rob: It was only the beginning, Dan. A few years ago, Guy Rossi, a partner in Nexus Financial/Lincoln Financial Advisors, asked Sam and me if we would be open to meeting with Emrich Stellar, who then introduced us to ESG. Emrich got involved, and we developed business succession and estate plans for Susan and the owner of one of the other companies she also owned as a partner. This opened the door for the day Susan announced, "I am thinking about selling my business, and I have a buyer that has offered me $30 million." I explained that I had access to your firm, which follows an exit planning process and could initially provide a complimentary MARKETABILITY ASSESSMENT to evaluate whether $30 million was a reasonable offer. We brought your partner,

Emrich, in to meet with Susan, and from there the process took off. Everyone involved made this a great team effort! We became Susan's team that helped maximize value and get the sale across the finish line.

Dan: Emrich, how did you approach this business exit engagement?

Emrich: I have been working closely for years with Nexus, providing training and support on business owner cases. Rob and Sam introduced me as the "out of town specialist with a briefcase" to their long-term owner who initially was a "stay and grow" business owner. We approached Susan with a Business Intelligence Insti-

> **"You'll never know what someone is willing to pay you until they come up against someone who can write you a bigger check!"**

tute [BII] engagement. She wanted us to provide comprehensive business and estate planning advice. As we guided her through the BII 6-STEP PROCESS, she grew confident about her personal financial resources and business readiness and become emotionally prepared to exit her business. As Rob mentioned, Susan garnered interest from a potential buyer who contacted her directly. She received an unsolicited offer of $30 million for the business she owned. Of course, this was nonbinding and a long way from a done deal.

Dan: Did Susan change her initial "stay and grow" objective and want to pursue a sale at this price?

Emrich: She was definitely intrigued! However, we advised her to go further and follow our exit planning process at ESG to make sure that she was maximizing value and had a high degree of certainty that a transaction would actually close. I counseled, "You'll never know what someone is willing to pay you until they come up against someone who can write you a bigger check!" She agreed, and so we began. After our in-depth analysis of the business and its financial statements, we engaged our preferred investment banking firm to help with the desired transaction.

Some of What to Expect Once You Receive an Offer
by Emrich Stellar, ESG Mid-Atlantic Regional Partner and BII Specialist

When selling your company, it is always exciting if there are multiple bidders driving up the value through a competitive auction process. However, we learned a long time ago that an offer is far from a closed transaction. Many business owners are often contacted by competitors or private equity groups that may be there in earnest, but they may also be on a fishing expedition for insight and information about a company, industry, or market.

The game really begins once you negotiate and sign a formal letter of intent (LOI). Our role is to help our business owners understand the twists and turns that are going to be ahead of them throughout the selling and due diligence process. They need to know what to expect so that when challenges arrive, they are prepared to address them calmly and professionally.

Early on we educate our owners on the fact that the current state of the art requirement to consummate deals often includes a quality of earnings (Q of E) report. The Q of E is typically performed by a national or large regional accounting firm that is independent of the client's company accountant. This report verifies, in an objective manner, the true earnings of a company. We have observed that both sellers and buyers are obtaining Q of E reports in modern deal activity. This is important to address because the cost can be anywhere from $30,000 to $150,000.

Due diligence is a very detailed process, like undergoing an executive physical; every area of the seller's business is poked and probed. This is a process that you do not want to go at alone. It is even more important if the LOI includes a purchase price based on a multiple of rolling EBITDA. It will be incredibly important to run your company well right up until the moment it closes, while also dealing with the relentless inquiries of the buyer's due diligence team.

Having your own exit team led by a quality investment banker and financial advisor will ensure that the process will stay on track and that you won't miss any deadlines or milestones. The challenge is that buyers often look to wear down a seller, which can lead to a bad result. If the seller loses momentum, the buyer can start to re-trade the deal and offer a lower price. The buyer will bring in their accountants and lawyers, whose goal is to justify their existence and fees. The buyer can use the other advisors in a "good cop/bad cop" approach to try to knock down the price. The buyer may even try to circumvent your exit team and say, "You don't need to work with those guys—we get along and can work this out together." Do not let that happen.

It's important to remember that most business owners are first-time sellers up against professional buyers—particularly when there is a private equity group or a consolidator on the other side of the table. They are looking to get the best deal possible, and it will be at your expense if you don't have a seasoned deal team to prepare you for this grueling final stage of the selling process and the gamesmanship that will happen along the way.

Throughout this process, there will also be negotiation over the structure of the transaction, such as a stock sale or asset sale, just as there will also be negotiations over the purchase and sale agreement. These have enormous income tax implications, and you need your exit team to know the rules of the road and how to maximize a give-and-take process. In addition, there will be negotiations over representations and warranties. The buyer may want the seller to hold back some of the purchase price to be sure the company operates as it has been purported. Again, you need seasoned advisors on your team to be sure that any money held back will be received at the end of a predetermined period through negotiations during the due diligence phase.

There may also be an offer to have one or more of the owners stay on with the company and accept rollover equity. This could give you ownership in the buying entity and potential upside value. This also has income tax implications, as well as lifestyle implications post-transaction.

The key to the selling process is to understand it before you start. If you have clarity about what could come up, then you will not be surprised when it inevitably *does* come up. The most important thing is to have seasoned professionals on your exit team to help you get to the finish line!

Dan: Doug, what happened after ESG brought you and your investment banking team into the process?

Doug: We quickly learned that Susan owned 100% of the company that she initially wanted to sell. We then found out that she owned 50% of another related company and 100% of a third smaller company. The 50% partner of the second company wanted to retire and be bought out. As we dug deeper and understood the connectivity and synergies shared by these businesses, *we showed Susan how much she could sell the original company for as a standalone entity and compared that to how much she could realize if she sold all three companies.* Susan quickly concluded that it would be far more advantageous to sell all three of them together, and her partners agreed! The MARKETABILITY ASSESSMENT we created with ESG, based on $20 million-plus gross revenues and EBITDA [earnings before interest, taxes, depreciation and amortization] of $7.25 million, yielded a valuation range of $35 to $37 million. Susan hired us and we went to market.

Dan: What challenges did you face initially?

April: It took months to get clean financial statements! We helped the owners and their CFO normalize their books and records, identify intercompany transactions, and prepare them for due diligence. As you know, owners are often underprepared to go into due diligence with a buyer. They think they will just give the buyer some financial statements and tax returns and be okay. In this case it took a fair amount of work to accomplish this task. We also needed to help the company make sure that its contracts and other records were complete and that they had the fully executed copies.

Dan: Eric, how many potential buyers did you approach?

Eric: Our strategy was to market the company to as many potential buyers as possible, making sure that we did not leave a stone unturned.

This is a once-in-a-lifetime event for an owner, so we want to make sure we get the best outcome available at that time in the market. In that regard, *we identified 213 target companies that we felt would have a strategic interest in acquiring this consolidated business*. Of these, 79 were eliminated by the owner, reducing the number to 134 who received our teaser and a nondisclosure agreement to sign. Ultimately, 31 signed and returned the NDA and received our confidential information memorandum [CIM]. This resulted in seven *indications of interest* [IOI] with a wide range of potential values. Of those, we invited the top three to meet the management team and have dinner afterwards. Susan felt extremely comfortable with a particular strategic platform company backed by a private equity group. We negotiated a formal LOI and started due diligence with them. The final buyer initially valued the company in the low $40s range but through tough negotiation and creation of competition, we ultimately closed at $55 million!

Exiting? Ask Yourself These Essential Questions

Before embarking on your exit strategy, make sure you have the answers to these key questions:

1. Do you know how to realize maximum value? Are you familiar with the "competitive auction" process of selling a business?

2. What is your exit time frame? Are you doing all you possibly can to position your business for sale at maximum value when you are ready? What have you done to plan for minimal exposure to taxes when you sell?

3. What would happen to your business if you were unable to show up to work tomorrow? Would it be able to go on? How would your family and your employees be impacted?

4. Do you have a family member to whom you would like to pass your business on?

5. What have you currently done to prepare your business and successors for the time when you decide to step down?

6. Do you have any formal documentation or a written strategic plan as to what you would like to happen to your company in the future? When was it last reviewed?

7. Have your existing advisors discussed exit planning, your preferred timing and strategies to enable this to happen successfully? Or have they been silent?

8. In your mind, how long do you think it takes to prepare so that you can leave your business?

9. As you consider leaving your business, what keeps you up at night?

10. When you no longer come to work every day, what will you do with your time?

Dan: How did you maximize Susan's "take home pay" from the sale?

April: Well, the buyer tried to pull a fast one and lower the price at the 11th hour, but we wouldn't stand for it. *From a tax planning standpoint, we also ensured that §1202 and a "late S-Corp election" option were thoroughly analyzed so the owner's C-Corp business would get the best income tax treatment available.* §1202 allows a seller to exclude up to $10 million of gain on the sale of stock. There are various requirements to be met for C Corporations: stock must be issued after August 9, 1993; taxpayer must have acquired the stock at original issue. It must have been held for more than five years; and the corporation must at all times have gross assets of $50 million or less. *These strategies saved over $1 million in taxes.* Additionally, a "gross up" to the sale price was negotiated for our owner's two S-Corp businesses to cover incremental taxes associated with the §338(h)(10) election filings. As with all ESG transactions, tax minimization is important. I know that you consider many strategies, such as Qualified Opportunity Zones, oil and gas programs that generate IDCs (intangible drilling costs), and depreciation to offset capital gains, charitable remainder and lead trusts, incomplete gift nongrantor trusts and other sophisticated techniques.

Dan: Emrich, what was Susan's reaction, and what post-sale implementation occurred?

Emrich: She was both pleased and relieved to sell her business! We satisfied Susan's "value gap" and helped her to achieve financial independence. We have helped with the investment of $22 million of sale proceeds. As part of her overall estate plan, we helped her acquire seven estate preservation life insurance policies to protect her family. We were also referred to her former 50% partner and several key employees to help with *their* financial planning. We have created a ton of goodwill. We are positioned as the most trusted advisors for business owners. We follow an unbiased process with our owner's goals in mind, and we have access to the right planning tools and the transaction capabilities of ESG and its investment banking partners. That's our "secret sauce"!

Dan: Thanks, guys. You were a pleasure to work with. You negotiated the LOI and financial terms of the purchase agreement, and they helped Susan save a tremendous amount in taxes. Any way you cut it, that's a real triple-play win!

Key Takeaways

- Don't wait until you're ready to go to the beach! It's a long process, and proper preparation and professional representation is essential.
- Don't ever accept the first offer. You'll never know what someone is willing to pay you until you find another suitor who can write you a bigger check.
- Follow an exit planning process that begins with a MARKETABILITY ASSESSMENT to ensure that you get top value for your business.
- Get your financial statements straight and prepare them for a rigorous due diligence process with an aggressive PEG buyer's attorney and due diligence advisors.
- Consider income tax strategies at both the company level and the personal shareholder level to reduce the IRS's share of the sale proceeds.

Chapter 7

"Going Up?" Elevator Deal Closes for Twice Initial Valuation and More...

As owners of an industry leader in the design, fabrication, and installation of elevator cab interiors, Jim and John bootstrapped their business in 2001, becoming partners after they had worked in the elevator industry for several years as mechanics. As owners, they made a good living but did not know how to build a transferable business until they connected with Matt Roberson and Derek Ferriera (ESG West and BII Specialists). Things got better from there, and they were soon able to sell 75% of their company for a cool $20.5 million—twice the initial valuation—and are on track to sell the remainder in a few years for $40–$60 million!

Objectives
- Sell 100% of the company for $9–10 million.
- Sell to key employees.
- Retire comfortably.

Challenges
- Business was initially dependent on its owners to run day-to-day operations.
- Owners learned that selling to their key employees was not their best option.
- Initial feedback from the market was not very positive.

- EBITDA fell by $1 million and initial buyer dropped their offer.
- Selling partners were not always in agreement on acceptable price and terms.

Interview Excerpts

- Dan Prisciotta, CFP®, CPA*, PFS, ChFC®, CBEC®, Managing Partner, Equity Strategies Group (ESG)
- Matt Roberson, CFP®, CBEC, ESG West Regional Partner, C Solutions
- Derek Ferriera, CFP®, CLU®, ChFC®, REBC, CBEC, ESG West Regional Partner, C Solutions
- Mark, Preferred ESG Investment Banker

Dan: This deal is another one of those that turned out exceptionally well for the business owners we assisted. Matt, you were there at the beginning. Can you provide us background on the company and how this engagement started?

Matt: It would be my pleasure, Dan. Our owners' company was an industry leader in the design, fabrication, and installation of elevator cab interiors. The two partners, Jim and John, bootstrapped their business in 2001. They had worked in the elevator industry for several years as mechanics and decided to join forces. Once the company got going, they were making a good living, but they did not know how to build a transferable business until they attended a seminar given by Derek Ferriera and me for ESG and the Business Intelligence Institute [BII].

Dan: Excellent. I imagine that your seminar changed their trajectory for the better.

Matt: It did indeed. Shortly after that seminar they retained Derek and me to help them grow and prepare their business for a future exit. We were able to help them learn how to build a proper organization chart and hire the right people to fill much-needed positions as project managers, and hire a COO to structure their company to be less dependent on their being hands-on with everything. With our assistance they developed a merit-based executive bonus plan to retain and reward their key employees, along with a defined benefit plan and a buy-sell agreement funded with insurance to protect the business and the partners' families in the event of a catastrophe—all growth concepts that would later become integrated into the Business Intelligence Institute approach. Accordingly, in not that much time their firm was elevated from a "mom and pop" to a thriving business that was less dependent day to day on them. Jim and John even learned how to enjoy longer vacations as they delegated more, and soon they were well positioned to sell.

Dan: Matt, you and Derek clearly were instrumental in helping your owners increase their business value. But let's backtrack for a minute. When you met them, what was their ultimate goal for themselves and the future of their business?

Matt: Their goal was to build the business up to a point where they could sell it and realize $9–10 million of value. Initially, they wanted to sell to their key employees. So we did a test run, and the owners concluded that an internal sale was not their best option. We pivoted to an outside sale and reached out to you to walk them through the ESG process and introduce them to ESG's platform of approved investment bankers.

Dan: Yes, I remember it well. As is our practice at the outset, we jointly prepared our MARKETABILITY ASSESSMENT, which showed a range of potential value between $9.4 million and $11.7 million. We then dove deeply into the results and potential strategies with Jim and John, and all agreed that one of our preferred investment bankers, Mark, would be the best fit for this engagement based on the owners' industry, size, type of transaction desired, and geographic proximity. Another factor in choosing Mark was that we had seen outstanding results with his firm on several prior transactions.

PEG Recap Provides "2 Bites at the Apple"
By Derek Ferriera, ESG West Regional Partner and BII Specialist

A recapitalization is **a transaction which results in the reallocation of the debt and equity in the capital structure of a business.** It represents an attractive option for owners considering an exit because it lets them exchange a portion of their equity for cash and position the company for future growth. It typically includes a private equity group (PEG) as an investor or partial owner in the business.

As stated elsewhere, one of our two owners was interested in participating in the upside because he is bullish on the future of his business and industry and desires ongoing involvement post-transaction. Owners who like to have a hand in seeing the company reach a new level of success find this option appealing. Given the addition of financial and intellectual capital a well-selected sale partner may bring, this can add a new level of financial success, as well as spiritual satisfaction.

Lastly, this method of exit can provide an excellent financial hedge for an owner, taking a portion of their financial risk off the table for all their years of arduous work. It also allows for upside to satisfy other goals to benefit their family legacy or community philanthropy that a single bite of the apple may not allow for. If the business growth strategy turns out as planned, the second bite can be significantly larger than the first!

Dan: Mark, can you give us a quick summary of the process you employed in this effort?

Mark: You bet. We took the business to market after finishing up the prior year's financial statements and projections. Our initial buyer list included about 200 targets, which we approached over a six-month period. This resulted in 55 signed NDA's [nondisclosure agreements] from prospective buyers requesting a copy of our deal book. The initial feedback from the market was not too positive, with feedback such as "the business is too project-based, "too local," "too tied to the ups and downs of construction industry," "all employees were union," and "too much customer concentration." Nonetheless, we persisted and received two letters of intent [LOI]. The first was for $14.5 million, which was fair, but we felt we could do better. The second offer initially came in even lower—$12.5 million—but we negotiated it up to $18.7 million.

Dan: Well, that definitely showed progress.

Mark: Yes, but then trouble hit: The company's EBITDA [earnings before interest, taxes, depreciation and amortization] fell by $1 million, and the buyer dropped their offer to $16 million. So, we dismissed them and went back to the market and found five new buyers, four of which were in the $16–17 million range. We then located a private equity group and pushed them to a $20.5 million offer, consisting of $14 million in cash plus a $4 million note and $2.5 million in rollover equity.

Dan: That's more than double Jim and John's initial value expectation!

Mark: Yes, and we negotiated the selling price as a multiple of the *single highest one-year* EBITDA they had ever achieved, not an average of the prior three years! There was lots of emotion and personality on both sides of the table. Even the partners were not always in agreement as to the acceptable price and terms, but we got it done! Having Matt and Derek as their advisors was very valuable. The owners trusted and appreciated their counsel and leaned on Matt a lot toward the end of our process.

> **"We negotiated the selling price as a multiple of the single highest one-year EBITDA they had ever achieved!"**

Matt: Thanks, Mark. It was our pleasure to help Jim and John exceed their goals. Needless to say, they are extremely happy! In addition to the $4 million of pension assets we were already managing, they have invested an additional $10 million with us: $2 million went into a variable annuity to provide guaranteed income for life, $1 million was invested into an oil and gas program for immediate tax benefits, and $7 million went into a managed assets program for long-term growth.

Top 10 Reasons Why Buyers Pay a Premium Price

It is often said that beauty is in the eye of the beholder. Buyers prioritize the attributes they seek based on their strategies and skill sets. These are the 10 most valued elements by professional buyers. ESG seeks to uncover these during our initial analysis leading to our MARKETABILITY ASSESSMENT. How many of these boxes does your business check?

1. **Owner's readiness to exit:** Your willingness to transition and follow an orderly timeline. ESG offers a Business Exit Readiness Index (BERI) to help you determine your financial and emotional readiness.

2. **Less owner dependence and a strong management team:** The presence of strong, skilled, and proven leaders who are willing to grow the business and capable of growing it in the future. Owners who have invested in bench-strength talent are often rewarded with premium values. ESG offers a tool to help you measure your business's dependence on you called Owner Dependence Index (ODI).

3. **Differentiated products or services:** A unique product or service that has intellectual property or a prominent brand is highly valued by buyers. Similarly, if customers view your company's products/services as unique or must-have, they tend pay a premium price.

4. **Strong market position:** A dominant position in a niche market or unique capability that provides differentiation is a characteristic of a highly valued business.

5. **Recurring revenue model:** Buyers place a premium value on consistency of historical performance. Customers with long-term contracts or proven recurring revenue provide stability. The ability to weather economic choppy waters with minor performance swings provides comfort to buyers.

6. **Scalability of your business:** Buyers seek segments with proven and projected high growth rates, so a company's systems, processes, and people are valuable to growth-oriented buyers. Owners who have invested in processes and systems for scalability receive higher values.

7. **Diversified customer/vendor relationships:** Concentration of just a handful of customers or suppliers adds risk to a buyer. Diversification is clearly a plus.

8. **Revenue growth:** History and prospects for future organic growth and available acquisitions that have been identified or are ready for action provide a glide path to prosperity. A skilled investment banker sells the future picture for the buyer.

9. **Gross margin and EBITDA margin:** These measurements, along with strong profitability relative to the market, are obviously important to buyers. Again, it is important to showcase past success, but even more critical to paint a rosy future. An expert investment banker will know how to sell based on projections that support the story of your business.

10. **Strong accounting systems and reliable data:** Without these, due diligence will be even more of a challenge. Once a buyer tenders a letter of intent and begins to diligently peek under the hood, they need to feel confident that your systems and data are reasonably accurate.

Dan: What does the future hold for Jim and John?

Matt: Well, Jim is looking forward to playing lots of golf, spending time with his grandchildren, and buying a second home in Hawaii. John has more time to fly his airplane and enjoy his place in Lake Tahoe. They thought they wanted to retire completely, but after they saw the deal that Mark put together, they decided to work for three more years to grow their remaining 25% interest and sell the company for $100 million. John continues to be involved in the business and is excited for his second bite of the apple. The post transaction has both good and bad news. The pandemic has slowed down the timing of the intended second exit. The good news is post-COVID projections increased the valuation to $40-60 million from the initial sale of $20 million, paying off handsomely for John taking on the second bite of the apple in the recap!

Dan: This is a perfect example of a private equity recapitalization, where business owners can sell a portion of the business while retaining some equity in order to take advantage of future growth. In this case, Jim and John cashed in some of their chips, took $18 million off the table, and will receive a second, hopefully larger, bite at the apple later. Derek, what lessons did you learn?

Derek: First, keep your options open. Initially, Jim and John thought they wanted to sell the business internally to their management team. As time went on, they came to their own decision to sell to an outside buyer. Second, work on your business prior to considering an exit. Do everything you can to focus on value drivers that pertain to the reasons buyers will pay a premium price. Third, have your exit planning advisory team in place and be ready to go. Jim and John had a solid accountant already, and we introduced a local high-end M&A deal attorney to work with us and our extremely capable investment banker to get the best outcome for them!

Dan: Thanks, guys, for another job extremely well done. The process works!

Key Takeaways

- When selling your business, keep your options open! You may have a preference for an optimal buyer, but that may change in a way that is very lucrative for you.
- Work on your business value drivers prior to considering an exit.
- Have your professional exit planning advisory team in place and be ready to go when the time is right.

Chapter 8

Owner Achieves Optimal Full-Price Deal, Saving $1 Million in Taxes

Andrew, owner of a successful commercial cabinets firm, was ready to exit, but he wanted to make sure his employees—especially his key person—were well taken care of. He had done an outstanding job of building a transferable business and already was able to spend plenty of time on his hobbies. He retained Business Intelligence Institute (BII) specialist Ryan Haag to prepare a comprehensive financial and business succession plan. Despite a drop in EBITDA during the marketing period, we achieved an all-cash, full-price deal, of which 98% was taxed at lower, long-term capital gains rates through a negotiated allocation. We also deferred taxes on the business real estate sold for overall tax savings of $1 million.

Objectives

- Sell business while retaining key person post-sale.
- Ensure financial security for spouse in the event of owner's death or incapacity.
- Make sure that the right buyer is brought in to keep the business intact.
- Keep everyone employed with the company post-sale.
- Ensure that the business stayed in the local community and did not relocate.
- Achieve favorable tax treatment for seller.

- Determine how much was needed from sale of the business (net) to achieve financial independence. The business was Andrew's personal piggy bank. Could he and his spouse maintain their lifestyle without the business?

Challenges

- Customer concentration of 60–65% from one source.
- Company attorney initially tried to overengineer confidentiality agreements that no buyer would ever sign.
- Forecasted EBITDA dropped precipitously during negotiations to sell.
- Owner had never had a team of advisors before and was losing sleep when his business experienced a downturn.
- The desired buyer did not originally make the highest bid.
- Andrew wanted to sell his building; however, his basis was low and he was facing a huge capital gain tax bill.

The ESG Team

- Dan Prisciotta, CFP®, CPA*, PFS, ChFC®, CBEC®, Managing Partner, Equity Strategies Group (ESG)
- Ryan Haag, CFP®, CEPA®, AEP®, CLU®, ChFC®, REBC®, RHU®, LUTCF, Traditional Wealth Management
- Dan W., Preferred ESG Investment Banker

Dan P: Congratulations, Dan! Thanks again for working with us to help Andrew achieve his vision of financial independence. We were able to achieve an all-cash business sale for him, including the sale of the company's real estate, along with $1 million in tax savings!

Dan W: I liked Andrew immediately when you introduced us, and I really wanted to help him achieve his objective to sell the company while retaining his company's culture and providing a future for his key employee. We achieved an all-cash deal, of which 98% was taxed at lower capital gains rates through a negotiated allocation. This move alone saved him $600,000 in taxes!

Dan P: That is really impressive considering the challenges you faced.

Dan W: Yes, this case was challenging for a number of reasons. To begin, buyers were concerned about his customer concentration of 60–65% from one source. On top of that, the company's forecasted EBITDA [earnings before interest, taxes, depreciation and amortization] dropped precipitously due to an awful start to 2019 with the financials barely at breakeven. *But* we managed to keep full price and close the deal based on the previous year's actual trailing 12-month [TTM] EBITDA. Without us, any buyer would have cut the price by at least $1 million because of the decline in EBITDA from the time of signing the letter of intent [LOI] to the closing date. They also would have demanded an earnout or deferred payments of some kind, which would have transferred risk to Andrew. But in the end, we got Andrew over $10 million all cash at the closing table. In addition, Ryan advised Andrew on how to accomplish a Section 1031 exchange for the sale of his business real estate to save even more taxes.

> "We achieved an all-cash deal, of which 98% was taxed at lower capital gains rates through a negotiated allocation. This move alone saved him $600,000 in taxes!"

Dan P: Ryan, you were there at the very onset of this exit plan. How did your relationship begin with Andrew?

Ryan: My buddy joined Andrew's company and quickly became his key person. I gave him your first book, *Defend Your Wealth.* He gave it to Andrew along with a note and my contact information. Andrew immediately emailed me, and I came in and met with him and his wife. They were looking for an advisor to help them financially organize and figure out their value gap. He was especially concerned about what his business was truly worth and how he would be able to replace the cash flow and personal expenditures that it paid for. Andrew originally wanted to work for three more years and then have his management team buy him out over 10 years. After completing your survey to determine his Business Exit Readiness Index [BERI] he inquired about selling to an outsider in case he died prematurely. ESG conducted a MARKETABILITY ASSESS-

MENT, and the results showed that a sale in excess of $5 million would satisfy Andrew and his wife Jill's value gap. He then engaged the services of my firm to take full advantage of our planning process and coaching, financial, and investment support services. Financial modeling was critical! We created an advisory team along with a BDO accountant and corporate attorney.

Dan P: Let's go back to Andrew's objectives. He had lots of toys and time to enjoy them. What motivated him to sell at this time?

Dan W: His wife, Jill, who is not active in the business, was afraid that if something happened to him, she would be stuck and have to liquidate the business for pennies on the dollar and probate the estate. Also, he wanted to make sure that the right buyer was brought in to keep the business as is, keep everyone employed, and keep it in the local community.

Real Estate and Taxes

Many of our clients own real estate beyond their personal residence. They own all types of investment properties, such as multifamily houses that they rent out, commercial buildings, raw land, industrial buildings, and other income-producing real estate.

Today's sky-high real estate market has caused many to consider selling, and some are bombarded with unsolicited offers at prices they could not have imagined just a year or two ago.

Excitement to sell sometimes gives way to the pain of the tax bill that will be owed. Depreciation deductions taken over the years reduce your cost basis dramatically, resulting in a significant tax liability upon sale. Long-term capital gains taxes can take 20%, and depreciation recapture may be taxed at 25%. Add in state income taxes, plus 3.8% net investment income tax on certain sales, and the total tax loss quickly approaches one-third of the selling price! Fortunately, there are ways to defer and possibly avoid these taxes.

How to Defer Capital Gains Tax on Real Estate Sold

Section 1031 of the Internal Revenue Code provides an effective strategy for deferring capital gains tax that may arise from the sale of business or investment real property. By exchanging the real property for "like-kind" real estate, owners may defer taxes and use the proceeds to purchase replacement property. Like-kind real estate includes business and investment real property, but not the property owner's primary residence.

It is important to note that there are several specific guidelines that must be followed in order to successfully execute a Section 1031 exchange transaction. For instance, the cash invested in the replacement property must be equal to or greater than the cash received from the sale of the relinquished property. In addition, the sum of the cash invested and the debt placed on the replacement property must be equal to or greater than the sum of the cash invested and the debt placed on the replacement property. In other words, additional cash can make up for a shortfall in debt placed on a replacement property, but additional debt cannot make up for a shortfall in cash invested in a replacement property. You should consult your tax advisor regarding a Section 1031 exchange prior to execution.

DSTs Are the Partial Ownership Structure of Choice

A Delaware Statutory Trust (DST) permits fractional ownership where multiple investors can share ownership in a single property or a portfolio of properties, which qualifies as replacement property as part of an investor's 1031 exchange transaction. A DST can be owned by a resident of any state. A DST takes all the hard work of being a landlord out of the hands of investors and places it into the hands of an experienced DST sponsor. This could be an excellent vehicle for tax deferral and tax-advantaged income for an investor in real estate who wants to be hands-off.

Investors with Property to Exchange

A typical Section 1031 exchange involving the eventual investment into a DST has three basic steps, shown in the figure below:

STEP 1

Exchanger sells property, known as the relinquished property, and proceeds are escrowed with a Qualified Intermediary (QI)

STEP 2

Qualified Intermediary, through a written agreement with the investor, transfers funds for purchase of replacement property

STEP 3

Exchanger receives beneficial interest in DST

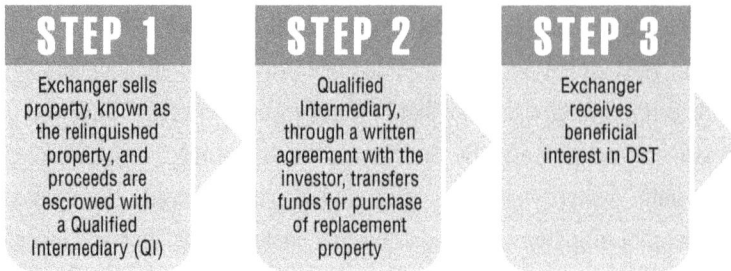

Key Benefits of DST 1031 Exchanges

Following are the key benefits for this type of exchange.

+ **No management responsibilities:** The DST is the single owner and agile decision maker on behalf of investors.

+ **Access to institutional-quality property:** Most real estate investors can't afford to own multimillion-dollar properties. DSTs allow investors to acquire partial ownership in properties that otherwise would be out of reach.

+ **Limited personal liability:** Loans are nonrecourse to the investor. The DST is the sole borrower.

+ **Lower minimum investments:** DSTs can accommodate much lower minimum investments, often as low as $100,000.

+ **Diversification:** Investors can divide their investment among multiple DSTs, which may provide for a more diversified real estate portfolio across geography and property types.

+ **Back-up plan:** If for some reason the investor can't acquire a specific property they identified to purchase, a secondary DST option allows them to meet the exchange deadlines and defer the capital gains tax. It is prudent to identify a DST on a schedule with your qualified intermediary if other properties you intend to purchase fall through. It happens!

+ **Eliminate boot:** If you fall short on a Section 1031 exchange, any remaining profit on the sale of your relinquished property is considered "boot." This remaining money becomes taxable unless you defer it. The excess cash can be invested in a DST to avoid incurring tax.

- **Swap until you drop:** The DST structure allows the investor to continue to exchange real properties over and over again until the investor's death. Thus, the capital gains tax can be completely avoided.
- **Estate planning:** All Section 1031 exchange investments receive a step-up in cost basis, so your spouse and children will avoid capital gains tax liabilities. A DST also provides them with professional real estate management versus the burden of hands-on management.

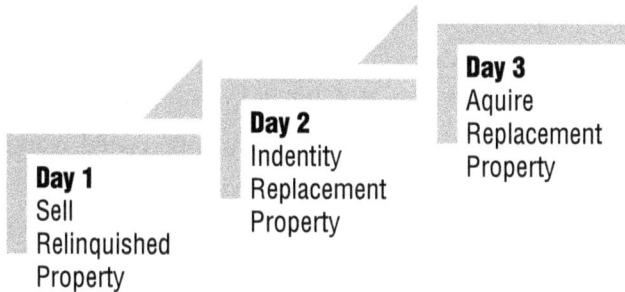

Day 1
Sell
Relinquished
Property

Day 2
Indentity
Replacement
Property

Day 3
Aquire
Replacement
Property

1031 exchange 180-day timeline

Like-Kind Real Estate

To complete a successful Section 1031 tax-deferred exchange, the replacement property must be like-kind to the relinquished property. Some examples of like-kind properties include:

- Multifamily apartments
- Healthcare
- Self-storage facilities
- Retail centers
- Industrial warehouses
- Student housing
- Senior living
- Hospitality

Any real estate held for productive use in a trade or business or for investment purposes is considered like-kind. A primary or secondary residence would not fall into this category.

Dan P: A major aspect of this transaction was the tax planning. This put a lot of extra money into Andrew's pocket. How did you achieve a 98% long-term capital gains tax treatment?

Dan W: We were able to negotiate the allocation. As an asset sale with an S corporation, we limited the buyer's ability to write up the assets, other than through goodwill. In other words, we compelled the buyer to allocate the majority of the purchase price to goodwill, achieving that 98% long-term capital gains tax treatment. We agreed on the fair market value of assets, close to book value, which resulted in very little taxable gain. Keep in mind that Andrew's CPA did not initiate this, so we took the lead during negotiations. We also really appreciated working with Ryan. He was able to help iron out issues with the company's attorney, who fought us at first. That attorney tried to overengineer confidentiality agreements that no buyer would ever sign. It ended up that he delegated the transaction to another attorney in his firm, who took guidance from us and was a good team player.

Dan P: Any other challenges?

Dan W: Yes. During the process, we also brought up options of selling internally to the 5% owner/key person, with our ability to arrange financing. They had looked at that before engaging us and thought that it was not possible. We informed Andrew that it *was* possible, and he felt better about bringing in an outside buyer to work alongside of his key person. He was happy this internal sale option was thoroughly explored, and he made his own well-informed decision.

Do You Manage Your Business Like an Investment?

Your business is one of the largest investments you will make in your life, so you need to treat it as such if you wish to one day exit with maximum returns. Here are some important points to consider (and to discuss with your financial advisor) as you shape your company for that big day.

- How much is your company worth? Has it been appraised in the last three years? Have you had a MARKETABILITY ASSESSMENT?
- What has been your shareholders' rate of return on investment in the business over the last one, two, three, four, or five years or more? How does this rate of return performance compare with other alternative investments?
- What portion of your net worth is tied up in your business ownership interest?
- Is your wealth adequately diversified to avoid the risk of major loss from adverse events with any of your assets, including your business?
- Does your business make distributions in excess of those necessary to pay taxes? If not, is the return on your investment of earnings into fixed assets or working capital sufficient to warrant the investments?
- Are you reinvesting distributions into nonbusiness assets investments as part of a plan to diversify your wealth? If not, why not?
- What is the plan to extract liquidity from your ownership of your business? And for your other shareholders, if any, to obtain liquidity from their investments? Is the plan realistic? Is it documented? Is it workable in the event something adverse happens to you, your partner (if any), or another key person?
- Is your business ready for sale? In other words, even if you did not want to sell it today, is the business positioned to be attractive to a wide range of prospective purchasers?
- Are there things you know that need to be done and that will take time to begin to put your business in a position to be ready for sale? What are they?
- What is the plan to transfer ownership and/or management to other members of your family, if that is your chosen exit path? Is this plan realistic? Is it documented?

Dan P: What type of selling process did you follow? How many potential buyers did you contact?

Dan W: We decided not to do a full auction with strategic buyers. We only went to specific financial buyers because they likely would not move the facility and would retain the key person. A strategic buyer would likely have moved out of the community and may have created an uncertain future for the key person and all employees. We contacted over 200 buyers, including private equity groups, family offices, and select wealthy individuals. We sent out more than 40 books and received eight indication of interest letters for acquiring the business. This led to five management presentations of four hours each.

Dan P: How did you move that to the next phase?

Dan W: We ultimately received three letters of interest, and Andrew decided to sell to someone who was not even the highest-dollar offer! The buyer was a wealthy individual who sold another business and originally had offered a much lower amount. We negotiated him up to $10 million, which Andrew felt was an acceptable level. That was a very good thing, because Andrew felt this gentleman was the best fit for the key person and the future of the company.

Ryan: The net result was that Andrew felt very good about his decision to sell to the buyer he selected. He felt we were extremely objective and explored the possibility of an internal sale as well as an external sale. He had never had a team of advisors before and was losing sleep when the business experienced a downturn. He was able to gain financial clarity due to our financial models and our leadership throughout the process.

Dan P: What are your takeaways from this process?

Ryan: Going through the ESG process was a great experience for all! We were super successful in managing all of the advisors so that they worked together smoothly and effectively, even in the face of the challenges that inevitably occur on the road to a highly successful sale. Psychology is important! It also was incredibly gratifying to see how much Andrew received net after taxes, because I know another business owner who sold on his own, just using his attorney and CPA *without* planning and negotiating the price allocation, only to get hammered with the tax results. We subsequently worked with Andrew and Jill on a

Section 1031 exchange of their real estate. Additionally, I worked with the key employee, who reinvested his 5% into ownership of the new company and was very happy!

Section 1031 of the Internal Revenue Code allows the owner to avoid paying capital gains taxes by reinvesting sale proceeds in a property or properties of like-kind nature and of equal or greater value. This saved another $400,000 in taxes.

Dan P: Thanks Ryan and Dan W. for all of your hard work and leadership on behalf of our clients. Andrew and Jill are on to the next chapter in their lives. They are enjoying the full rewards for building and selling their business (and real estate) to a new owner who, along with their key person, will continue their legacy and benefit their community as well.

Key Takeaways

- Assemble an exit team that will work well together under stress.
- Achieve clarity through rigorous financial modeling and what-if scenarios. Visualize future cash flow to feel confident about life post-sale.
- Plan carefully and creatively for the most favorable tax treatment for the sale of your business and real estate with an S-Corp asset sale and by allocating the premium amount of the purchase price to goodwill.
- Choose an investment banker best suited to your objectives.
- Follow the process and remain patient.
- Plan ahead to defer capital gains taxes on business-related and investment real estate through the use of Section 1031 "like-kind" exchanges, and consider a Delaware Statutory Trust (DST).

Chapter 9

Telling the Story a Different Way to Reach $20 Million

Charles owned a medical equipment manufacturing company and a medical services company—two businesses that typically do not coexist under the same roof, due to the unique attributes of their respective healthcare-focused business models. Accordingly, the service business was profitable while the manufacturing side lost money. This, combined with a number of accounting issues, previous unsuccessful sale attempts, declining valuation, and Charles's strong and sometimes aggressive personality, made marketing the company very challenging. ESG connected Charles with Allan, our preferred investment banker, who had previous success in healthcare M&A and deep knowledge of the healthcare industry. Allan crafted the story to the M&A marketplace a different way—one that attracted the ideal buyer and produced a great result.

Objectives
 ✦ Sell two closely tied businesses together—a service business that was profitable and a manufacturer that was losing money.

Challenges
 ✦ Owner was unsuccessful at three previous attempts to sell his companies.

- Initially only able to find a buyer who was interested in the service business alone.
- Company underperformed the projections they had previously put out into the marketplace through their prior investment bankers.
- Business had three contracts that comprised 35% of its EBITDA, and the contracts were terminating in six months.
- Uncovered accounting irregularities that extended the due-diligence process, which dragged down value and impacted the buyer relationship.

The ESG Team

- Dan Prisciotta, CFP®, CPA*, PFS, ChFC®, CBEC®, Managing Partner, Equity Strategies Group (ESG)
- Allan, Preferred ESG Investment Banker

Dan: Allan, congratulations! You and your team helped us accomplish a Herculean task. I know it was a particularly difficult engagement, and we appreciate your tenacity and hard work to get this deal done for our owner, Charles. When we first contacted you regarding this opportunity, we discussed your qualifications as the best fit for this particular engagement. The company is in the healthcare industry and in a very specific niche. What experience did you and your group bring to the table?

Allan: As we explained to Charles at the onset, our company indeed has deep experience in the healthcare industry. We had recently sold a hospice company, a medical equipment company, a chain of senior living facilities, and a behavior health company. So, this opportunity was right down the fairway for us. We had the ability to aggressively market the company to a wide range of domestic and foreign strategic buyers, as well as private equity groups with related platform companies.

Dan: And that's exactly why we introduced you to the situation. Share with us what challenges you faced as you worked through this transaction.

Allan: As you will recall, Dan, knowledge of how medical insurance companies reimburse providers was necessary to understand the companies' business model. Charles's companies were unique in that he was both a manufacturer of the machine that provided a special type of therapy and also a service provider of that therapy. All of the other companies in the industry do one or the other, not both! Focusing on manufacturing *or* providing service was the common wisdom in the market. Initially, the goal was to sell both companies. We quickly learned that the manufacturing company was losing money, while the service company was profitable. That made it very difficult to get a buyer interested in the manufacturing company.

Dan: As evidenced by the fact that Charles tried to sell his business before our involvement and failed miserably.

Allan: Yes, he had previously hired three other investment bankers to sell his company between 2006 and 2013. They all claimed to be high-powered industry experts; however, they couldn't get a deal done! They did get some offers, but none of the offers were satisfactory. A second challenge was that the company underperformed the projections they had previously put out into the marketplace through their prior investment bankers. That obviously presented a difficult set of facts to manage. The final challenge was a customer concentration issue. The business had three contracts that composed 35% of its EBITDA [earnings before interest, taxes, depreciation and amortization], and those contracts were terminating in six months.

Dan: Charles was eager to sell. He did not have any family to take the reins. He had a younger wife who wanted him to get out of the business and retire, plus he was feeling burnt out and at his age was experiencing some health problems.

Allan: Yes, he was motivated, but nonetheless threw every obstacle in our way. It was difficult to find a buyer because of all of the previous unsuccessful efforts. Since it was a niche market, many of the possible buyers had previously been approached and turned the deal down. We had to convince folks to take another look. *We had to tell the story a different way.*

Dan: Tell us more about that.

Allan: Sure. Several of these industry buyers had taken a look at this deal before and had dismissed it. However, when we brought it back to them, we pointed out the certain advantages that they hadn't previously seen, and as a result they saw the appeal. We emphasized unique aspects of the business's competitive positioning, manufacturing flexibility, and service model that others hadn't considered, and this provided the motivation that buyers needed to take another look at the opportunity. Those who met the owner learned that his was a difficult personality. So, we took a focused rifle-shot approach rather than a broad shotgun approach. We researched and put together a buyers list with less than 100 potential companies with which we wanted to maintain utmost confidentiality. We received indications of interest from a dozen buyers. Three potential buyers got serious, and ultimately the buyer was a private equity–backed management team. The president of that team had run a similar company, sold it, and wanted to get back into the game. He had looked at many deals and had two other options besides this one, but we got him focused on working things out with Charles.

"We had to convince folks to take another look. We had to tell the story a different way."

Dan: So, you *were* able to find that one buyer who was primarily interested in the service business, and then motivated that buyer to put an attractive offer on the table for both businesses. The offer was so compelling to our client that he ultimately accepted it. In fact, you brought in the highest multiple ever received.

Allan: Absolutely, but there was even more adventure to come, Dan. Once we found the buyer, due diligence uncovered a number of irregularities regarding the seller's method of revenue recognition, transferability of contracts, accounting for property taxes, and so on. Normally a 30- to 60-day process, due diligence dragged on for many months due to these issues. This delay led to a downward adjustment to EBITDA and caused the relationship between Charles and the buyer to deteriorate.

Maximize Value Drivers; Minimize Value Detractors

When preparing and marketing your business for a sale, ESG's professional advisory team will take a look at what may be holding you back from getting maximum value, and what you can do about it. Regardless of your business situation, there are always actions you can take to maximize your value drivers while minimizing the detractors. Following are some factors in that all-important equation.

VALUE DRIVERS

* **Positive financial trends:** In virtually every instance, the company's financial performance will be one of the single largest drivers of value. Thus, it is very important that the company show strong performance in revenue growth, gross profit, and operating profit.
* **Unique product or service:** The more differentiable the company's products and services, the greater the perceived value. "Me too" businesses do not trade at as high values as companies with unique or proprietary products, services, and capabilities.
* **Low customer concentration:** Too much revenue concentrated with a small number of customers is viewed as risky by buyers, as there is concern with what happens if one or more of the company's key customers are lost. This concern translates to lower valuations.
* **Competitive positioning:** Competition is a reality for most businesses. The better positioned a company is relative to the competition, the higher that company's value will be.
* **Multiple suppliers:** Buyers do not like a company to be overly dependent on any one vendor. A company that has at least two suppliers for each key product or service will be viewed as less risky, and thus more valuable, than a company that only has one supplier.
* **Low owner dependence:** It is common for buyers to be concerned that a business is overly reliant on the owner. Having a strong non-owner management team in place will help reduce the perception that the

business may suffer without the owner's involvement and will thus help improve value.

VALUE DETRACTORS—Beware of Major Risks

Sometimes value can be created by reducing or eliminating those elements that decrease value. Buyers measure a company's attractiveness partly by the *absence* of value detractors.

- **Owner dependence:** As noted above, a business that is overly dependent upon its owner(s) for managing the business, generating sales, or other key functions is often viewed by buyers as less attractive, unless there is a layer of senior management in place that could take over these responsibilities or a clear path for a new manager to take over. The more willing an owner is to remain involved with the business for a reasonable transition period, the more comfortable a buyer will be.

- **Customer concentration:** Revenue concentrated with one or a few customers is a top value detractor. Respondents clarified that most would not purchase a business with customer concentration greater than 40% (and they would be concerned at 25%).

- **Poor accounting practices:** If a company has questionable accounting systems and controls, buyers will quickly lose confidence. This is why buyers will often request a quality of earnings study to test the numbers as part of their overall financial due diligence.

- **Low or declining gross or EBITDA margins:** Both gross margins and EBITDA margins (cash flow to service debt and growth) are usually compared to other acquisition opportunities and the company's prior performance.

- **Cyclical or declining industry:** Declining industry trends greatly impact M&A demand and pricing. Owners operating in cyclical industries need additional planning and consideration on timing market cycles and an owner's transition.

- **Union workforce:** This is a particularly big factor if you have recent or anticipated issues with the union.

- **Environmental issues or unresolved lawsuits:** This can be an especially significant value detractor if exposure exists or is uncertain.
- **Heavy capital expenditures:** These include outlays for equipment and working capital to continue growth, usually defined as more than 5% of revenue or 20–50% of EBITDA.
- **Supplier dependency:** This comes into play when you have a single source for critical materials, parts, or services, or at-risk foreign sources.

Dan: How did you manage to overcome all of the challenges you faced with this deal?

Allan: Pure tenacity! Weekends and nights on the phone with the buyer. Never giving up. Three or four times, the buyer threatened to walk. We had a very contentious dinner at a restaurant with the buyer and Charles, which resulted in yelling and Charles storming out! Nonetheless, we worked tirelessly to maintain a constructive deal atmosphere and keep things moving forward. But we hung in there and managed to get the deal done.

Dan: What role did ESG and the owner's financial advisor play?

Allan: The advisory team did an excellent job as advocates of the deal, since it was what the owner wanted. You all kept Charles focused and on track. There's an old saying that "time kills all deals," and with the lengthy due diligence process, it was difficult to keep everyone on track. This deal would not have happened if it were not for the relationship and the respect that Charles had for his advisor.

Dan: Wow. How does this long and winding road of a story end?

Allan: Well, aside from achieving the high multiple in the industry, we had a very happy ex-owner! Probably even more important, his wife was delighted because they would be able to spend more time together. The key objective had been met. After building the company for 44 years, Charles walked away with a substantial amount of cash and began really enjoying his life. He also was able to bask in the comfort that the legacy of his business would continue and his key employees would be protected as a result of our successful negotiation to secure jobs for all of his key people.

Dan: Thanks, Allan, and congratulations again. One major takeaway is that as advisors we should put all exit options on the table for our owners. At one point, this could have been a family succession case or an ESOP, but Charles chose a third-party sale. Second, hire the most tenacious, creative investment banking firm you can find. Third, it's important for the owner and financial advisor to stay very close throughout the process.

Key Takeaways

* When hiring your M&A advisor, remember that while knowledge of your industry niche can be important, the character, tenacity, creativity, and capabilities of the investment banking team is what will get you to the finish line.
* Consider multiple exit options as suggested by your advisor.
* Hire the most tenacious, creative investment banking firm you and your advisors can find.
* For a business with a difficult history, find a way to tell the story a different way that will resonate with your potential buyer.

Chapter 10

Targeted Auction Boosts $40 Million to $62 Million

Larry and Blake were partners in a manufacturing company serving the aerospace, automotive, life sciences, and general industrial products industries. At 53 and 64 years of age, they had no formal exit plan—just the general idea of "we will sell when the time is right." Larry was content to keep working, but Blake already had one foot out the door—he was spending a lot of time enjoying his hobbies. When one of their largest customers expressed interest in buying and happened to be a great fit, they knew the time had come! Their Lincoln Financial Services (LFS) advisor, Paul Solorzano, advised them to call ESG and the process took off from there. Thanks to a targeted auction, the buyer's initial $40 million valuation turned into a sale for over $60 million!

Objectives
- Sell company for maximum value.
- Sell to a company with a similar culture and geography.
- Enjoy the proceeds in retirement.

Challenges
- Owners had particular requirements for price and type of buyer.
- Preferred buyer initially wasn't highest bidder.
- Preferred buyer tried to reduce price at the last minute.

The ESG Team

- ◆ Dan Prisciotta, CFP®, CPA*, PFS, ChFC®, CBEC®, Managing Partner, Equity Strategies Group (ESG)
- ◆ Paul Solorzano, CFP®, Sagemark Consulting
- ◆ Allan, Preferred ESG Investment Banker

Dan: Paul, tell us about your relationship with the owners. How did it begin?

Paul: Larry was a referral I received about 10 years ago from one of my first clients. They grew up playing football together. Larry is married with three young children, and when we met, he and his wife had done very little personal financial planning. I produced a comprehensive fee-based financial plan for them. That resulted in the establishment of an investment portfolio, 529 education plans for their children, and a total of $10 million of life insurance to support a cross purchase buy-sell agreement. Larry's partner, Blake, has one adult son he tried to bring into the business, but it did not work out. About five years prior to this exit, I produced a plan for Blake to clean up his estate situation and put together an investment strategy. Both men have pilot's licenses and owned airplanes as a way to develop and retain business.

Dan: How did Larry and Blake get started in the business together?

Paul: They met while working together at another company that went bankrupt. They pooled their pennies and bought the equipment from the bankrupt company, which eventually became their manufacturing business over 15 years before this deal took place. They started with nothing, and it took them several years to gain momentum. They could not have dreamt it would grow into an entity they could sell for $62 million!

Dan: Well, the result was better than a dream, obviously! So, what made these owners finally decide to go forward with selling their company?

Paul: They had always told me that they would sell when the time was right, probably when Blake turned 70. However, they also stated that given the right offer they would sell sooner. They were constantly approached by business brokers, private equity groups, and strategic buyers to sell, but they never took any of the offers too seriously. Then they were approached by one of their biggest customers, a publicly traded company that expressed a real interest in buying their firm.

Dan: That must have gotten them off the dime, Paul. What happened then?

Paul: The truth is that Larry was not ready to sell, but he recognized Blake already had one foot out the door, playing golf and flying his plane—and while Larry may have been able to run the business on his own, he didn't have an interest in effectively being a solo business operator. In addition, both partners felt the company had maxed out its growth opportunities, and to enter new lines would take a serious commitment of time and capital. With a legitimate suitor pushing to buy, they knew that in order to get the best price possible, they needed help. So, I recommended ESG to them. Being prudent, they did their due diligence and checked around for who else might be able to help them do the sale right. Ultimately, as a result of the fact that I had become such a trusted advisor, they decided to engage with ESG, and we set up an appointment with you!

Dan: Thank you for that, Paul. We started the process with a Zoom meeting in which we focused on getting a deeper understanding of the owners' goals, time frames, and company details. After a 90-minute data-gathering session and a thorough review of their firm's financial statements, ESG prepared its Marketability Assessment. Based on their industry and type of transaction desired—which was selling to a strategic buyer with a similar temperament and geographical location— we introduced them to Allan, one of ESG's preferred investment bankers. Allan has significant experience in the manufacturing sector. Further, ESG and Allan had completed a successful transaction a year earlier. Allan and his firm also had been awarded Strategic Deal of the Year by the M&A Advisor—the preeminent M&A organization in the industry. So, we were extremely confident in Allan's capabilities.

Paul: Larry and Blake and their CFO and outside CPA agreed with the results of ESG's complimentary Marketability Assessment that

$40 million was a reasonable value based on $20 million gross revenue and a multiple of six times EBITDA of $6.5 million. At the time, typical multiples for this type of company fell in the range of five to seven times EBITDA. However, they were looking for a price above $50 million. One item that motivated them to hire Allan was his flexibility to alter his firm's standard engagement agreement to add incentives for any sales price above $40 million. With the flexible fee arrangement, the owners agreed to retain Allan and his firm, whose strategy was to employ a targeted auction approach. Aimed at buyers that had been prequalified, this would utilize more of a rifle, rather than a shotgun, approach to the marketplace.

The Strategic Advantages of a Targeted Auction

- Limited exposure to the marketplace protects confidentiality.
- Increases the seller's negotiating leverage with the best potential buyers.
- Potentially accelerates transaction timeline with greater deal velocity.
- Seller maintains greater control of the flow of information.
- Creates competitive environment and sense of urgency among buyers.

Dan: What happened next, Allan?

Allan: We did our industry research, leveraged our knowledge of these types of companies, and developed an initial list of about 50 strategically identified buyers. Several months of hard work resulted in 15 indications of interest, which led to six management presentations. And so, the targeted auction progressed. In the end, we circled back to the public company that initially approached Larry and Blake with an offer of $40 million, which was unsatisfactory to them. The buyer asked me where they needed to be in order to win the competitive auction. At that point I told the preferred buyer their final offer "needed to have a 6 in front of it." Of course, they had no idea what the other offers were, and through our research and analysis we knew that it was important that they not risk losing the deal to a competitor. Thus, the buyer stepped up and raised their offer significantly, to a price of $62 million!

Dan: Fantastic result! Of course, there always are challenges. What were yours?

Allan: This transaction wasn't easy given the sheer number of bidders and the owners' requirements on price—plus, Larry and Blake wanted a strategic buyer in a similar geographic area. Obviously, the auction worked out extremely well, and we were able to get the number we needed, but even then, there was a last-minute issue: The buyer tried to change the terms of the deal just prior to closing, but we wouldn't allow it! I believe that this buyer knew it was paying a premium for the business and wanted to see whether we would stand our ground on the deal terms. We didn't budge and achieved a great outcome for our owners!

> "Of course, they had no idea what the other offers were, and through our research and analysis we knew that it was important that they not risk losing the deal to a competitor."

I Know Who My Buyer Is. Why Do I Still Need an Investment Banker?

It is not unusual for business owners to be contacted by industry participants and/or private equity groups interested in buying their company. For these buyers, entering into single-party negotiations is to their advantage, as there is little or no competition in these situations and the seller has less negotiating leverage as compared to a traditional M&A process. In an effort to dissuade business owners from hiring an investment banker, buyers may say some interesting things, including "We don't negotiate." The reality is that, while buyers may *prefer* not to negotiate, they will do whatever it takes to buy attractive businesses that add value.

Professional buyers complete numerous transactions each year, whereas for most business owners, the sale of their company is the first time that they have gone through this process. Without representation, business owners who pursue unsolicited offers are often unfortunately outmatched. If you are a business owner considering a sale, you should have an investment banker in your corner. An experienced investment banker will help the business owner level the playing field and will run a process that results in a better outcome to the seller. The investment banker will position the seller to optimize the terms of a transaction, increase competition, improve the seller's negotiating leverage, and manage the process to ensure a smooth and timely closing.

In my many years of representing business owners, we have worked with a number of companies that have received unsolicited offers. In every instance, we were able to achieve a better outcome for the seller either by negotiating an improved deal with the original buyer or by attracting another buyer that made a more attractive offer. For most business owners, the sale of a company is one of the most important financial transactions of their life. In order to optimize the outcome of this important transaction, it is important that every business owner have an experienced team representing them.

Dan: Paul, what can you say about the job that Allan and his firm performed for Larry and Blake?

Paul: In the first meeting with Allan, Larry and Blake brought along their CPA. Coincidentally, the CPA knew of Allan and his firm. The CPA's son, a corporate attorney, had just finished working on a deal with Allan that ended very well. This gave Allan and his group instant credibility. When the deal was almost done, I asked Larry if engaging Allan had been the right decision, especially since it was he and Blake that had brought the ultimate buyer to the table. Without hesitating, Larry said, "Allan earned every penny we paid him. There is no way we would have sold for over $60 million without him!" The buyer who originally offered $40 million had said, "We don't negotiate." However, Allan negotiated brilliantly.

Dan: Yes, he did. From start to finish it took 18 months from the initial meeting and just four months once the letter of intent [LOI] was signed to close the deal. Allan was very patient with this engagement and did not rush to market until everything was ready. He had Larry and Blake close out the fiscal year, worked with their CPA to clean up the financial statements, and prepared an impressive marketing package before approaching any potential buyers. Allan then reached out to buyers during the second quarter of the following year. Once things got started, they moved quickly. What were the results of this transaction?

Paul: Larry and Blake paid off the note on their relatively new plane. I now manage a total of $30 million of their investments. Larry decided to stay on after the sale for two years. He is very close with his family, and both children are still in high school. Blake was looking forward to not working at all. He moved to Nevada to play golf, fly, and hang out with his buddies.

Dan: Very nice. What's your secret sauce, Paul?

Paul: I really feel that this case developed as it did because of our firm's "Serve First" philosophy—understand our owners' objectives, help educate them about their options, and ensure the plan is implemented! I try to do this with all my owners. In this case, it included flying from San Francisco to LA for quarterly reviews for years, providing them with a high level of service and helping each put his financial house in order. Of course, you and your team were central to this success story. I mentioned ESG's capabilities early, because you have always provided a phenomenal resource to my business owner clients.

Key Takeaways

- Explore and understand your objectives and your options for achieving them.
- Use the best sales strategy and process for your type of business and needs.
- Hire an investment banker, even if you think you have the best buyer on the hook.

- Work with an M&A expert with significant success in your sector.
- Think outside the box in pursuit of your preferred buyer, and rely on your team of financial and M&A professionals.
- Be patient, and you may far exceed your goals!

Chapter 11

Family Business Rejuvenated After Partial Sale

A leading family-owned shipping company with multiple locations across the U.S. was doing quite well until different objectives for the firm drove the clan apart. Emotions ran high, and the parents and their adult children could not agree on the vision for the company. The ongoing fireworks drove the family's decision to sell most of their company, and they changed course several times along the journey to exit and achievement of their goals. Their exit planning team devised a solution that would transform the family, grow the business exponentially, and provide freedom they did not know existed.

Objectives
* Sell the business in order to preserve family harmony.
* Create liquidity to start new business ventures.
* Diversify wealth—after years of focus and sacrifice, all of their eggs were in one basket.
* Allow each family member to pursue the business ventures best suited to their strengths and preferences.

Challenges
* Constant conflict caused objectives to change frequently.
* Like many good deals, this one cratered four times (at least!) before closing.

- Pandemic negatively impacted earnings and values during the deal process.
- Company continued to miss their projected EBITDA month after month throughout 2021 and into 2022, causing deep concerns among buyers.
- Investment banker contracted COVID-19 during negotiations.
- Accounting system crashed and valuable data was lost during the due diligence process.

Case Study Highlights

- Dan Prisciotta, CFP®, CPA*, PFS, ChFC®, CBEC®, Managing Partner, Equity Strategies Group (ESG)
- Joe Brezden, CLU, ChFC, CFBS, CRPC, CBEC and Michael Brezden, CFA, Brezden Wealth Advisors
- Mark G. and Mark J., ESG Preferred Investment Bankers

Dan: Joe and Mike, as the preeminent father-son team in the financial advisory business, how did you get started with this family?

Joe: We were in a networking group and met a commercial banker who introduced us to the family because their bank was concerned about their concentration of wealth in the family business and lack of liquid assets outside of the business to provide collateral for loans. During our initial meeting with the father, mother, son, and daughter, we learned that they had no buy-sell agreement to protect the business and themselves in the event one of the shareholders were to retire, die, become disabled, or involuntarily or voluntarily leave the business We were hired as their fee-based advisors and immediately went to work to design and fund the agreement with life insurance on the shareholders owned by a specific-purpose LLC.

Mike: We then designed their estate plan with new wills, trusts, powers of attorney, and healthcare directives. Then one day, the father and son showed up at our office and said, "We need to talk." There was lots of conflict within the family, even boiling to a point that almost led to a physical altercation. This tension drove their decision to sell the business. They also felt pressure due to lack of capital and the desires of various family members to go in different directions.

Dan: When they decided to sell, I recall their value expectation was $23–27 million. They had a valuation from their bank that showed a net value of $17 million in 2018. We performed our MARKETABILITY ASSESSMENT, which yielded a value in excess of $30 million based on their financial performance at that time. EBITDA [earnings before interest, taxes, depreciation, and amortization] had grown from $2.4 million in 2016 to $3.4 million in 2017 and $4.6 million in 2018, and it was projected to exceed $5 million in 2019. We selected our ESG investment bankers based on their industry knowledge, proven process, and track record of success. They connected very well with all of the family members and exuded professionalism and competence. The family was impressed—"grand slam" was what I heard! So they unanimously decided to hire Mark G. and his firm.

Dan: Mark G., what was your first order of business once the family retained you?

Mark G.: As we were gathering additional financial data to prepare our offering memorandum or book, the family had a meeting over the weekend, patched up their differences, and decided not the sell the business! Instead, they decided to hold on to it, grow it, and start a second business in a related field.

Dan: Yes, I recall that vividly. You came up with an excellent suggestion to help them achieve their new goals.

Mark G.: That's right. When the family decided to keep the business and develop an aggressive growth strategy, my idea was to help them accelerate their growth plans. I asked the founder, "How long do you think it will it take to achieve your new goals?" He thought for a minute and responded that it might take six or seven years. "What if we could reduce that time frame by two-thirds?" I asked him. They were all ears. "What if we can find a strategic partner who will invest in your business, alongside the family, to achieve a common purpose?" I showed them how they could take advantage of fresh capital to grow faster, take some chips off the table, reinvest, and ultimately cash out for a much bigger number!

Dan: So, the new objective was to identify and negotiate with several potential industry-experienced partners for a recapitalization— that is, sell off a portion our client's company, not the entirety. What happened next?

Mark G.: We went to work, Dan. We launched our marketing campaign and received over 50 NDAs [non-disclosure agreements/ requests for information]. Then in March 2020 the global pandemic struck. This put everything on hold until the world sorted things out.

Dan: Of course, that impacted a lot of transactions.

Mark G.: After several months, we were able to get back on track. We identified four excellent strategic partners for the family to evaluate. The first was a PEG [private equity group] focused on their industry. They had completed over 100 acquisitions, all in their specific industry, and would not micromanage the business, giving the family plenty of control. The second potential partner was also a PEG. They were from New York City and well-funded but they were "cold fish"—not the most dynamic personalities. However, the family liked them anyhow because they offered a high valuation and would be completely hands-off. The third was a strategic buyer in a related industry and was publicly traded. That one dropped out because they determined that they had other larger acquisitions in their pipeline that they wanted to pursue. The fourth potential partner was a wealthy family office. Culturally and philosophically the family saw them as a great partner.

Strategic Buyers versus Private Equity

When planning your exit strategy for a sale to an outside buyer, consider the respective benefits of strategic buyers versus private equity groups, and how they match up against your objectives and company attributes.

STRATEGIC BUYERS

Strategic buyers are larger companies that operate in your industry or one closely related to it. They have access to low-cost capital, abundant operational synergies, and the ability to leverage an acquisition through their sales channels. Strategic buyers pay premium values for the following three core elements:

- **Strategic fit:** Strategic buyers' corporate development departments have well-established strategic and acquisition plans. An investment banker with relationships and knowledge of their growth plans is invaluable. The development of a thoughtful acquisition thesis for each strategic buyer is essential to successfully court these premium buyers.

- **Synergies:** The ability to reduce costs with volume pricing is just one example of synergies a strategic buyer can bring to the table. Sophisticated buyers tell us these synergies only occur with their acquisition, but an investment banker skilled at running a competitive auction process motivates a buyer to share these synergies in the form of a higher purchase price paid to the seller.

- **Product line or services extensions:** Strategic buyers often look for M&A opportunities to augment their existing products or services and complement their business plans. An investment banker with strong industry relationships and awareness of a buyer's missing pieces can present the idea powerfully by proposing to fill product needs, geography gaps, or talent shortages by acquiring your company.

PRIVATE EQUITY

This category is also called financial buyers, made up of private equity groups, funds, and firms. These buyers look for platform companies that hold a solid niche in their desired markets. They invest in business and often allow previous owners to retain some upside in a transaction and have a longer transition with a qualified partner by acquiring a portion (either minority or majority recapitalization) of a business. Private equity buyers tend to focus on their rate of return and typically hold for three to five years, add value, and then sell. If an owner is ready to sell all or a portion now but is open to staying with the company for a period of time, selling to a PEG can be extremely advantageous.

Savvy investment bankers will often approach both types of buyers simultaneously to create a bidding war and to negotiate the best price and terms to give you the greatest flexibility and options.

Mark G.: One of the family office's members wanted to be on-site in the business, which the owners weren't initially thrilled about. But we felt that if his role could be narrowly defined, it could be an acceptable arrangement. Despite being everyone's favorite, their offer was the lowest, at $40 million, and included a significant earnout component. We pushed them to $44 million, but it was still too low for us to accept.

Dan: Around that time, I understand their accounting system crashed! They had to manually re-input all of their data. They also hired a CFO for the first time, who brought a wealth of experience and helped modernize their systems. While you created a tremendous amount of interest in this company, it wasn't all smooth sailing, was it?

Mark G.: All in, we received 68 NDAs and could have closed a transaction in 2021. However, the family had yet another disagreement. But we were able to bring everyone together and continue the process. I recall we had at least four stops and starts during the process due to internal conflicts, changes in the business, and growth spurts. It was difficult to keep potential buyers engaged, but we did it.

Dan: The family ultimately decided to accept a formal LOI [letter of intent] with the wealthy family office you brought to the table. You got them to increase their offer significantly as our client's revenues grew. We also learned that the family office was funded by five billionaire families who own the largest company in Central and South America in this industry, and our client's business would be their entrée into the U.S. market. What did you experience during due diligence?

Joe: We then found out that Mark G. had contracted a severe case of COVID-19. The family became concerned, and we reached out to you for guidance. Our clients did not want to lose the buyer and were a bit frantic. Should we find a new investment bank? Try to put the deal on hold? Your oversight of this case saved the day! You intervened with your knowledge of the process, our client's personalities, and their needs, and your problem-solving skills got us back on track. What a real value-add.

Dan: We had a family meeting to determine our next steps since we learned that Mark might be out of the equation for the remainder of the transaction to deal with the long-term physical effects. Fortunately, our investment bankers have a robust firm with bench strength, and I introduced Mark's partner and co-founder [Mark J.], who was able to step in and become the lead investment banker to bring it all home.

The LOI accepted included cash upfront of $70 million plus 20% rollover equity and the balance of $10 million in an earnout, for a total value of $100 million!

Mark J.: I jumped in and got up to speed very quickly. With my 25-plus years of deal-making experience, it didn't take long. The buyer brought in KPMG to perform a Q of E [quality of earnings] study, which flagged some revenue that they asserted was nonrecurring and overstated 2020 earnings. Earnings were off by $1.7 million. We continued to negotiate and maintain the high valuation we sought. The LOI accepted included cash upfront of $70 million plus 20% rollover equity and the balance of $10 million in an earnout, for a total value of $100 million! In addition, they received $5 million of excess working capital (cash on the books in excess of payables). With every obstacle we overcame, the value never changed. The deal structure evolved a bit, but the family received the same overall valuation and certainly way more than they expected. They had plenty of cash now to invest in other ventures, upside with the rollover equity, and reinstated peace in the family.

Joe: After the transaction closed, we met with the entire family. The energy and feeling in the room were palpable. They had previously felt restrained, as if they had hit a barrier and could not go any higher in their business for years…before they met us. They could not borrow any more money from the bank for growth and expansion. They had to turn down customer requests to open more facilities to service their needs. They were "growing themselves broke" and could not afford to expand further. Their son, the visionary, felt corralled and stunted. He wanted to create new projects related to but separate from the family business. This created tremendous pressure and conflict with the core business and his sibling. The recapitalization we helped achieve brought in a well-funded partner with industry knowledge and contacts, which is pushing the business to new heights! They have busted through the invisible barrier and are running free! It was as though a wave of energy was released. The son could now focus on new ventures (with his family as investors), while his sister continues to be employed by the core business with a lucrative employment contract for three years and options for them to renew.

Mike: Also, the company's operations and financial management have improved vastly. By growing through our exit planning process and learning what buyers and investors wanted, it forced them to "institutionalize" their company and create best practices, which will now serve them very well into the future. They buttoned up, created a stronger company, hired a CFO and other staff, and upped their game to another level. They told us the partial sale brought them freedom.

Joe: Repeatedly, the father would look to us as the guardians of the family and ask, "Are we going to be okay? Can I sleep well at night?" We looked him in the eye and said, "We got you!" He joked and replied, "I can die now a happy man." The humorous part is that he is the healthiest person we know and may outlive us all! This was not just a transaction for the family; it was a transformation!

Dan: That's fantastic! In addition to rolling over some of the sale proceeds into the new, larger company with the family office and funding their other business ventures, how are they managing their wealth?

Mike: It's interesting that our relationship up to this point focused so much on their business protection, business growth, and exit strategy that we had not fully discussed our investment management offerings. Frankly, they plowed everything they earned back into the business and did not have anything left to invest. Leading up to their liquidity event, they were introduced to a major national wire house and bank with lending and investment capabilities. They emphasized their past performance but did not impress the family or connect with them.

Joe: When we sat down and addressed their investment needs, we asked if they had benefited from the resources we brought to them thus far. This included ESG, Mark and Mark, the attorneys, and so forth. They responded with a resounding yes. We explained that we would handle their investments just as professionally and competently as we surround ourselves with our team at Lincoln Financial Advisors. In addition, Mike is a CFA [Chartered Financial Analyst] and quite adept at developing investment strategies for our clients. We described our local presence backed by national support and strength. We are not bank employees; we own our wealth management practice and follow an objective process with no conflicts of interest. We also have access to several lending facilities.

Mike: The family then told us that they hadn't fully understood that our firm provided these services at such a high level and were pleased to allow us to manage their new liquidity. We started off with $25 million and built a portfolio that will allow them to borrow up to 80% of their investments at very low interest rates. We think another huge win will occur in several years when they cash out again with their rollover equity as part of this potentially $1 billion company. What an outcome!

Key Takeaways:

- Embrace the collaboration that occurs between you, your financial advisors, and your investment banker/ESG.
- Stay persistent and flexible through any stops and starts. It will pay off in the end.
- Advisors need to have the emotional intelligence to ask the right questions, listen intently, and be totally owner focused. They need to understand, pay attention, and take the time to listen, respond, and advise the multiple parties involved.
- Be steady and don't overreact when frustration sets in. Find reasonable solutions to press on toward achievement of a common goal.

Chapter 12

Watch Out for the Third Rail!

Two brothers started a business together in the early 1990s, growing it into an award-winning manufacturer of architectural metalwork that was ranked on the Inc. 5000 Fastest Growing Private Companies in America. In 2019 they decided they wanted to take advantage of an optimal time for them to exit and maximize value. However, a close look at their books revealed some irregularities that threatened to upend their dreams—a third rail that sent 600 volts of electricity through the buyer's due diligence process! Fortunately, ESG, Kishore Mirchandani, and Kenneth Burack helped them overcome the issues, netting $70 million against an initial value expectation of $35–40 million!

Objectives
* Sell for maximum value.
* Ready to move on to the next chapter…start another business or invest in real estate.
* Gabriel was 51 and Isaac was 43 years old when they decided to exit. They were open to staying on for a while with the new owner.

Challenges
* Their "third rail" was the company's accounting practices. It sent 600 volts of electricity through the buyer's due diligence process!

- Market launched during global pandemic.
- During negotiations, EBITDA declined from $11.5 million to $9.2 million.
- Vendor concentration—90% of materials they purchase were from China
- 90% exposure to new construction.

Interview Excerpts
- Dan Prisciotta, CFP®, CPA*, PFS, ChFC®, CBEC®, Managing Partner, Equity Strategies Group (ESG)
- Kenneth Burack, CFP® BII Specialist
- Kishore Mirchandani, Financial Professional
- Kevin, Preferred ESG Investment Banker

Dan: The brothers, Gabriel and Isaac (50/50 owners), have been clients of yours for several years. I know that you helped them with their insurance needs and investment management. What is the story behind their business and decision to sell?

Kishore: They started together in the early 1990s, Dan, and through determined and savvy dedication had grown their firm into an award-winning manufacturer of architectural metalwork used in some of the most stunning buildings in America. For the last decade they were ranked on the Inc. 5000 list of Fastest Growing American Companies. They continued to excel during the pandemic and built a new facility in 2021 to bring their entire team under one state-of-the-art roof to serve their national and international list of customers. Even then, they didn't rest on their laurels, continuing to invest heavily in technology and machinery to increase productivity, gain market share, and reduce operating expenses. They minimized exposure to supply chain disruption by manufacturing more components in-house. Business was soaring, so they decided it was the optimal right time to exit!

Dan: That's an impressive story! At what point did you decide to collaborate and bring in Ken?

Kishore: Ken spoke at one of our firm's training meetings about his financial and estate planning process, and I was very impressed. He also discussed the Business Intelligence Institute (BII) and access to your firm, ESG. Afterward, I told Ken that my owners really need help. They did not have a buy-sell agreement for their business, worth approximately $20 million at the time, or a proper estate plan or exit strategy.

Dan: Ken, what did you initially encounter in this case?

Ken: As you know, I am very process oriented. I started by analyzing each family's cash flow and estate planning picture. We developed a plan to significantly reduce exposure to confiscatory estate taxes. We also designed their buy-sell agreement and implemented a supplemental executive retirement plan [SERP] for several of their key employees to reward and retain them. I recommended a specialized attorney to help draft the buy-sell agreement, wills, and trusts, and coordinated the entire process with Kishore, Gabriel, and Isaac.

Dan: What was their thinking regarding an exit plan?

Ken: They were all over the map. Their CPA had mentioned an ESOP, and they even considered an IPO at one point. Gabriel and Isaac had even engaged an investment banker a year before I met them, after interviewing several firms. It took a long time for them to compile data and go to market. When they finally started marketing the company, five parties showed interest, but then nothing happened. They did not receive any offers. These investment bankers flew several buyers in to tour Gabriel and Isaac's facilities before they negotiated any indications of interest [IOIs] or had any written offers whatsoever.

Dan: That's terrible! Our team would never subject a business owner to that treatment and potential breach of confidentiality without a written commitment!

Ken: Exactly, and I know that you were horrified when I told you that, and was 100% sure that you and your ESG team could get these guys on the right track. So, I encouraged them to meet with you. I also sent them a copy of your prior book, *One Way Out: How to Grow, Protect, and Exit from Your Business*, which they appreciated and read.

Dan: Yes, that initial meeting gave me the opportunity to gain a deep understanding of their business and objectives, as well as their different personalities—I learned that one brother was level-headed and business savvy, while the other was a bit volatile and enjoyed endless haggling and pushing the envelope! Then, when I conducted a financial statement analysis, it showed that their EBITDA [earnings before interest, taxes, depreciation, and amortization] was extremely lumpy over the years 2016 to 2019. It went from $3.4 million to $8.7 million, then down to $5.7 million, and was projected to be around $5.7 million again in 2019!

Ken: Yes, their case presented some challenges right off the bat.

Dan: Indeed. When we did our complementary MARKETABILITY ASSESSMENT, it produced a value range of $38–44 million based on capitalization of earnings, discounted cash flow, comparable sales in their industry, plus other factors. This was a rather tight niche—our initial research indicated approximately 100 PEGs [private equity groups] and only 92 potential strategic buyers. In the previous 24 months only 40 deals in this space had closed—13 by PEGs and 27 purchased by strategics.

Ken: And that's one of the reasons you introduced Kevin, ESG's preferred investment banker for this industry and type of transaction desired.

Dan: Correct. Kevin has a unique process designed to understand the buyer's reasons for acquiring a particular company and what additional revenue and profits they will gain through their acquisition, and he knows how to negotiate an "outrageous" price. Kevin, what happened after the owners retained you and your firm at the end of 2019?

Kevin: Dan, we started working on our confidential information memorandum [CIM] and reviewed it with Gabriel. He wanted to shine it up and add a lot of razzle-dazzle as if it were a brochure designed for a customer. I believe he learned this from the other investment banker, who created a lot of fluff and was ineffective. We had to convince him that buyers are accustomed to receiving information in a certain way and that we have a results-proven method of constructing our CIM. Too much glitz and the buyers may perceive that there is something wrong with the numbers and that we are trying to cover something up. Of course, we do not put the name of the company or a price in the CIM.

After several more meetings, we agreed on the content and style of the CIM and launched our marketing outreach with high expectations!

Dan: Good thing you were there to help do that the right way! So how was the marketplace reaction once you went forward with marketing the company?

Kevin: It was excellent! We instantly received over 50 inquiries with 40 signed NDAs [non-disclosure agreements] from potential buyers seeking access to the CIM and secure virtual data room. About 10 potential buyers reviewed and passed on the opportunity. There were two main reasons for this. One was exposure to new construction—90% of the company's revenue was new-construction related. The other was that the pandemic had just hit, and many companies were putting their acquisition pursuits on hold. Still, we got great traction. Sixteen buyers bowed out, leaving 32 interested parties. We increased the total number of NDAs to 65, with total buyer activity responding to our marketing efforts to 104. In total, 158 potential buyers looked at this company.

> We increased the total number of NDAs to 65, with total buyer activity responding to our marketing efforts to 104. In total, 158 potential buyers looked at this company.

Dan: And then you began to call for IOIs.

Kevin: Exactly. The first IOI came from a private equity group and was too low at $32 million. We continued to push to create a bidding war. We set a deadline for all interested parties to make offers. We then managed to attract two offers in the $60 million range, along with a foreign buyer, who was flying in for a visit. We continued to push hard via Zoom and in-person meetings. Multiple offers exceeded $60 million. However, several PEGs wanted Gabriel and Isaac to rollover $15 million into equity in the new company, and they were not comfortable with investing that amount. I held very firm during these negotiations to get the owners what they wanted, and they appreciated it.

Dan: Based on Gabriel and Isaac's objectives, how did you all choose the "best" buyer for them and their company?

Kevin: We had in-depth conversations with several potential buyers and performed our due diligence on them. I called for a final round among the top prospects to make their "best and final" offers within a strict deadline. We had additional visits from the three best potential buyers. But there were issues: EBITDA for 2020 was expected to be $11.5 million but came in at only $10.2 million. Then Gabriel informed me that after they closed the books at year-end it would actually be only $9.2 million. I told them our buyers will be concerned, and indeed, some of them tried to "retrade" their original offers. Meanwhile, Isaac was pushing me to ask for an $80 million price!

Dan: How did you manage that dynamic?

Kevin: Well, I kept talking with the three finalists to get them to understand the new EBITDA number and issue their LOI. My goal was to keep them above $60 million despite the significant drop in EBITDA. I successfully negotiated a LOI with an excellent private equity buyer focused on their industry for $70 million (consisting of $40 million cash at closing, a $10 million promissory note, and $10 million of roll-over equity into the new company, plus a $10 million earnout.) This was $10 million more than the second-highest offer plus significant upside potential, which Gabriel and Isaac desired!

> **"I successfully negotiated a LOI with an excellent private equity buyer focused on their industry for $70 million…This was $10 million more than the second-highest offer…"**

Dan: LOI accepted and off into due diligence we go…

Kevin: Correct. But we had detected significant accounting irregularities which needed to be addressed and corrected immediately. The company only did a closing of their work in process [WIP] once per year—as of December 31—so they only had an accurate cost of goods sold figure on *one day per year*. Buyers need to see WIP accounting performed every month. They will not be comfortable with financial statements that were accurate on only one day a year. In addition, supply challenges hit the business in early 2021, and Gabriel insisted they were fine but could not prove his profits existed. We had to bring in an outside CPA to close the books monthly and perform a Q of E [quality of earnings] study. The Q of E showed EBITDA of only $6 million through October, expected to rise to $8.7 million by year-end. Gabriel eventually saw the wisdom in doing this and was grateful. He also insisted on purchasing new equipment for $1.4 million, which greatly improved efficiency, reduced dependence on outside vendors, and made the business more scalable for a buyer. In fact, we ultimately negotiated hard with the buyer to pay the owners back half the cost of the new equipment since they will benefit from its use in the future.

Dan: How did Gabriel and Isaac respond during the due diligence phase?

Kevin: Well Dan, they were shocked by the amount of due diligence. It was almost overwhelming, but I counseled them to be patient as I steered the ship. Strained due diligence with a PEG is some version of hell on earth when the accounting is off. It took hundreds of hours to reconstruct their books and prove the accuracy of their numbers. This deal would not have happened without us, as evidenced by the failure of their prior investment banker to attract an offer. Due diligence with strategic buyers is not as tough as with a PEG. We also brought in a great deal attorney—he remained calm when emotions ran high with the buyer and sellers. When the buyer complained to me during due diligence, the attorney and I sorted out the issues between what was important, not important, and potential deal breakers. We kept negotiations on track and moving toward a favorable outcome for our owners.

Dan: Talk about challenges! Their transaction presented many roadblocks.

Kevin: Indeed. Gabriel and Isaac had never sold a business before. They were smart but inexperienced. They were wise to rely on their advisors, and they tried to be patient. We had sourced a very good buyer, who hung in with a sincere desire to pay Gabriel and Isaac the premium value deserved, and then keep them on as business partners after the closing.

Dan: How are you helping the brothers to manage their wealth?

Ken: We reran all of Gabriel and Isaac's cash flow models to show how they achieved their financial independence once the dust settled. Kishore and I earned a tremendous amount of credibility and trust by helping them throughout their exit journey. Even though Gabriel's daughter works for Goldman Sachs, they are in the process of investing with us into professionally managed real estate and marketable securities. Preserving wealth for their spouses, children, and future generations is also important to them, and we have established multiple spousal lifetime access trusts [SLAT] with dynasty provisions funded with permanent life insurance to provide multiple generations with asset protection, growth, and estate tax avoidance. We opened investment accounts for each of Isaac's young children to teach them how to invest at an early age, and the benefits of compounding, diversification, etc.

Dan: Excellent! So how did Gabriel and Isaac feel after completing this entire process?

Ken: This deal checked all of their boxes! The value received far exceeded their initial expectations of $35–40 million, and they feel the smartest move was maintaining a one-third ownership in the new entity formed with their company and its new private equity owner. Their buyer/new partner is an excellent strategic fit, and they are excited to participate in the growth of the new company over the next three to five years to get a second bite at the apple. They believe it could become $100–150 million. So ultimately, all of the hard work paid off, and we are delighted to have gotten them such a nice result!

Key Takeaways

* Don't let accounting be your third rail! Have a qualified independent CPA review or audit your financial statements to be sure they are prepared in accordance with generally accepted accounting principles so that you will chug along through due diligence.

- Build the best advisory team you can, and trust them.
- Don't be a know-it-all; rely on your advisors' experience, especially if you have never sold a business before.
- Hire good accountants and attorneys who are proactive and understand the due diligence requirements of buyers.

PART TWO

Sales to Employees

Chapter 13

Achieving Exit Success
With the ESOP Path

This chapter is a little different than those in the rest of the book. Its intent is to give you an overview of an exit path that for many unique reasons is showing exceptional growth in popularity: the employee stock ownership plan (ESOP). In the last few years ESG has closed more ESOPs than ever before, providing business sellers with surprisingly attractive valuations, along with other benefits such as minimizing capital gains taxes for selling shareholders, preserving company culture, protecting founders' legacies, improving high levels of motivation among employees, maintaining equity interest in future upside of the business, and more! In the following pages I offer an informative Q&A on ESOPs, and briefly summarize three recent ESOP sales that produced beautiful results for all involved.

Objectives
- Sell company for fair market value.
- Allow for continuation of company culture.
- Defer or avoid capital gains taxes.
- Maintain equity interest in future upside of the business.
- Increase employee retention and motivation.

Considerations
- ESOPs are complex.
- ESOPs demand specialized financial advisors and transaction partners.

- ESOPs are usually financed with a combination of outside debt (commercial banks, private debt funds, etc.) and seller notes.

Benefits
- Potential significant tax savings.
- Preservation of company culture while increasing employee retention and motivation.
- Maintaining an equity interest in the business.
- Certain ESOP-owned companies can operate without income tax liability.

Despite numerous benefits, employee stock ownership plans (ESOPs) are sometimes overlooked as exit and liquidity strategies. While the process of establishing and managing an ESOP follows a proven process, misinformation abounds. To sort out the facts, let's take a look at the following 10 most common points of confusion.

1. Are ESOPs only for S corporations?
Partnerships, LLCs, and C Corps also can be prime candidates. A partnership can be incorporated as a C or S corporation prior to the close of an ESOP sale. Existing corporations can also convert their corporate structure before formalizing an ESOP transaction in order to maximize selling shareholder and entity benefits. These decisions are carefully analyzed in order to determine the unique tax benefits for both companies and selling shareholders, as well as accounting implications. Optimal structures are company-specific and should be considered with guidance from ESOP and tax specialists after appropriate analysis.

2. Is employee ownership too complicated?
ESOPs are complex, but so are third-party and private equity sales. All transactions demand specialized financial advisors and deal partners. While there is a cost to maintaining an employee-owned company, such as annual valuations and debt service, the stakeholder benefits can significantly outweigh the downsides. Historically, any strategy that offers significant tax benefits requires a higher degree of complexity.

ESOPs are no different, but in the end, the benefits can easily outweigh the complexity.

3. Do selling shareholders receive adequate value?

ESOP transaction multiples are generally similar to what financial or private equity buyers would pay, depending on the industry. Trustees have a fiduciary responsibility to pay fair market value for a company's stock. The IRS defines fair market value as "the price that would be agreed on between a willing buyer and a willing seller, with neither being required to act, and both having reasonable knowledge of the relevant facts." I will say from experience that a competitive auction process run by a qualified investment banker could result in a selling price much higher than fair market value in specific industries. This needs to be weighed against other ESOP advantages. I have also seen situations in which a sale to an ESOP can provide the seller with future upside through warrants tied to the growth of the company.

4. What if employees don't have the money to purchase the company?

Employees do not pay out-of-pocket for shares. Even in a leveraged ESOP transaction, the sale is typically financed with a combination of outside debt (commercial banks, private debt funds, etc.) and seller notes (payments due to seller over time). This debt is taken on by the sponsor, not the employee trust. As the company pays down these obligations, shares are distributed to the trust and allocated to employees. Since the company (once the ESOP is completed) qualifies for significant tax deductions, if an S corporation, it becomes a non-taxpaying company, the interest and principal is repaid from the tax savings, typically costing the company nothing.

5. Can a leveraged ESOP put too much debt on a company?

A trustee is obligated to strike a deal in the employees' best interest. Unsustainable debt runs counter to that goal. An experienced ESOP advisor should analyze a company's present financial situation, balance sheet, future prospects, and ability to service debt under stress. If third-party financing is sought, loan underwriters will do the same. Banks that finance ESOPs typically apply the same degree of scrutiny as in other leveraged transactions. Seller debt is usually subordinated to outside lenders and is unlikely to apply undue pressure on the company's financial health. The tax advantages of a properly structured ESOP also must be considered. Applicable corporate income tax deductions help increase free cash flow and facilitate efficient debt repayment.

6. Do ESOP lenders require personal guarantees?

A: Many lenders are willing to negotiate financing without personal guarantees. Employee ownership transactions are generally attractive to debt providers. ESOP-related tax deductions can enhance corporate cash flow. Companies with solid financials and sufficient collateral should be able to secure nonrecourse financing.

7. Do sellers have any say in how an ESOP company is run post-sale?

Employee-owned companies are overseen by a board of directors. Even in instances where a company is 100% employee-owned, founders and former shareholders often hold board positions and continue to play integral roles and retain board control but have a fiduciary responsibility to act in the best interest of the company and employee owners.

8. Will employees gain access to confidential information?

Disclosure of sensitive financial statements to employee owners is not mandatory. While employee-owned companies may elect to share some data, plan participants are only required to receive annual statements pertaining to their individual accounts along with a copy of the summary plan description. These are similar to documentation provided for other qualified retirement plans. That being said, the more transparent management is with the employee owners post-transaction, perhaps the greater the employee buy-in of ownership mentality.

9. Do ESOPs prohibit family ownership?

Employee ownership can be a valuable tool in family succession planning. Multigenerational businesses can use leveraged ESOPs to create tax-advantaged liquidity events for certain family members and next-generation equity transfers for others. Family members employed by plan sponsors can also participate directly in an ESOP, under certain conditions.

10. Is ESOP ownership permanent?

ESOPs allow for broad flexibility post-formation. Employee-owned companies can engage in secondary ESOP sales, stock buybacks, plan terminations, and mergers and acquisitions). Plan trustees have a say in these transactions. Fair market value for plan participants remains a critical concept. But ultimately, a trustee seeks to act in the employees' best interest—even if that entails a sale to a third party later on.

Who Is the Ideal ESOP Candidate?
- Business owner who desires full or partial liquidity.
- At least 20 full-time employees.
- Business value of at least $5 million or net income of $1 million or more.
- Five-year track record of profitability.
- Solid second tier of management preferred to continue to run the company.

Benefits
- Allow for continuation of company culture and legacy in its hometown.
- Immediate sale of company stock (100%) or smaller percentages over time.
- Defer and ultimately eliminate capital gains taxes on sale to ESOP.
- Sell for fair market value plus maintain equity interest in future upside of the business.

- ESOP can increase employee retention and motivation, and provide eligible employees with significantly higher retirement benefits.
- ESOP-owned company can become 100% federal and state income tax-exempt (S corporation). Think about how much cash can be saved without the burden for the company to pay taxes every year! The freed-up cash may be used for multiple business-enriching purposes.

ESOP #1: ENGINEERING FIRM TAKES ANOTHER LOOK

Interview Excerpts
- Dan Prisciotta, CFP®, CPA*, PFS, ChFC®, CBEC®, Managing Partner, Equity Strategies Group (ESG)
- Derek Tuz, CFP®, ChFC®, CWS®, Aegis Financial Partners, BII Specialist
- Michael Cohen, CRPC®, CEBC®, BII Specialist, Sagemark Consulting

Michael and Derek consulted with ESG to determine if an ESOP was appropriate for their owner.

Dan: What can you tell us about this case, Derek and Michael?

Derek: The principal owner, Robert, was referred to me for a key person life insurance need. When we first spoke, I told him that I would be happy to sell him a large key person insurance policy, but that it was not the right thing to do. "You need a plan!" I told him. This resulted in a comprehensive Business Intelligence Institute engagement, through which I brought in Mike Cohen for his expertise.

Michael: As Derek and I gathered data, we asked Robert, "Have you ever considered an ESOP?" He responded, "Oh, we're too small, and we had a bad experience with the largest ESOP in our industry. They misused our prior employer's company 401(k) by converting it into company stock." I suggested to him that it still may make sense to explore it, and he agreed to take another look.

Dan: After our initial ESG interview and data analysis, we brought in our ESOP specialist firm to perform their ESOP Feasibility Study. In this case, Robert and his co-owners were not focused primarily on maximizing value; their objective was to benefit their 33 loyal, hardworking employees. As it turned out, the ESOP was a perfect fit!

Derek: Yes, it was! Robert received all of his cash up front when his company sold to the ESOP. The design utilized a 100% leveraged ESOP. As the company pays down the note to the bank, value goes up. Robert and his partners also received warrants, which we recommended they gift to a newly created trust to reduce their future estate tax liability by removing the warrants from their taxable estate.

Dan: Excellent result! What now?

Derek: Robert and his partners acquired much-needed life insurance to help provide liquidity to fund the ESOP repurchase liability and to pay off the bank loan if a selling shareholder dies. The insurance cash value also creates a sinking fund or reserve to help pay for living buyouts or employees retire or leave the company. This worked out extremely well for all involved. Like I always say, "Believe in the Lincoln Financial Network process—Serve First!"

ESOP #2: CONCRETE CONTRACTOR TRANSFERS OWNERSHIP TO 250 EMPLOYEES

Interview Excerpts

- Dan Prisciotta, CFP®, CPA*, PFS, ChFC®, CBEC®, Managing Partner, Equity Strategies Group (ESG)
- Mark Bronfman, MBA, CPA, BII Specialist, Bold Value Partner

Dan: Mark, I recall that you first met Jerry when you were engaged to set up an executive compensation program for his company and assist with his estate planning. How did that proceed?

Mark: The 57-year-old owner was considering his exit strategy and had 250 employees, so I suggested exploration of an ESOP. Jerry's objectives were key: honoring the perpetual legacy of his company and maximizing value to the selling shareholder.

Dan: That's when we brought in our preferred ESOP specialist, and the design got very creative.

Mark: Correct. Jerry had expected his business to be worth $18 million. Our initial preliminary valuation came in between $23 million and $27 million with a midpoint value of $25 million The closing ESOP value was ultimately $34 million + $2.6 million in positive adjustments (cash to seller, post-closing adjustments) for a total of $36.6 million.

Dan: Another fantastic finish!

Mark: And that wasn't all! In addition, Jerry received warrants that could yield another $9 million down the line! Lesson learned: In the right circumstances, an ESOP can be the best buyer *and* the best new owner.

ESOP #3: UTILITY AND SITE DEVELOPER EXCEEDS VALUE EXPECTATION AND SAVES ESTATE TAXES

Interview Excerpts

- ◆ Dan Prisciotta, CFP®, CPA*, PFS, ChFC®, CBEC®, Managing Partner, Equity Strategies Group (ESG)
- ◆ Rick, AIF, CRC, Managing Partner of Preferred ESG ESOP Specialist Firm

Dan: A CPA close to Jim's company referred me to discuss ESOPs. I told him about our ESG exit planning process and transactional capabilities, including ESOP, and he thought it would be a perfect fit. So, we got together, and I laid out the ESOP process and the benefits of Jim going in that direction for his exit.

Rick: And that's where we came in.

Dan: Yes. I introduced Jim to you to analyze the possible ESOP we had been discussing.

Rick: Indeed you did. We conducted ESG's complimentary Marketability Assessment (ESOP Feasibility Study) in this case, which conservatively put Jim's company in the $23 million to $28 million range. Jim was very enthusiastic about that outlook, but we ended up exceeding even those expectations when the ESOP sale closed for a cool $40 million!

Dan: Fabulous! And there were other benefits as well. Jim will also stay on and earn additional retirement income—exactly what he wanted! In addition, he received warrants, which have a low value today, ideal for estate planning. These were transferred to an irrevocable trust as a gift for almost nothing. Appreciation will occur outside of his taxable estate. In addition, his management team received stock appreciation rights [SARs], which will increase in value as a result of their efforts which are a great motivator!

Rick: Life must be good for Jim now!

Dan: For sure. He has upgraded to a 72-foot Viking yacht and will enjoy more time sport fishing in the Gulf of Mexico!

Key Takeaways

* Request that your professional team evaluate the merits of an ESOP as one of your exit planning options.
* Allow an ESOP consultant or M&A professional specializing in ESOP implementation to help you evaluate whether an ESOP would be an acceptable exit and liquidity option, even if that structure didn't seem feasible in the past. Circumstances change.
* Consider the significant benefits of avoiding capital gains taxes through an ESOP sale.
* If employee retention and recruitment, protecting the company's legacy, and preserving your company's culture are driving goals, an ESOP may well be the best "One Way Out" for you.

Chapter 14

There's Not Just One Way Out... There Are Multiple Doors to Choose From

Dealing with the unexpected can create challenges, but there's always a solution. Betty and Roger, the owners of a successful construction firm with 60 employees, had long assumed that their exit strategy would be family succession, but when the time came, tragedy struck and the heirs apparent were rendered incapable of taking over. On their own, they then explored a sale to outsiders and a management buyout, neither of which turned out to be feasible. They were considering liquidating the company when Michael Cohen of Sagemark Consulting suggested an ESOP as their exit vehicle, culminating in a creative $10 million sale that checked all the succession boxes.

Objectives
* Satisfy immediate need for liquidity.
* Ensure financial security during retirement.

Challenges
* Was not feasible to sell to children, outsiders, or senior management team at the company.

- Needed to educate owners on the advantages of an employee stock option plan as an exit strategy.
- New federal legislation meant educating a new commercial banker on nuances of Small Business Administration ESOP lending.
- ESOP trustee halted work on the transaction when the pandemic hit.
- Original commercial banker departed during loan process.
- Company had outstanding PPP loan.

Interview Excerpts

- Dan Prisciotta, CFP®, CPA*, PFS, ChFC®, CBEC®, Managing Partner, Equity Strategies Group (ESG)
- Michael Cohen, CRPC®, CEBC®, BII Specialist, Sagemark Consulting
- John and Matthew, Preferred ESG Investment Bankers

Dan: Mike, how did you first start working with these business owners?

Mike: I met Betty 25 years ago. She and her business partner, Roger, started running a division that had spun off from Betty's family construction company. They grew the business over the years and were very employee-centric. Betty and Roger fostered a great corporate culture over many years of harmoniously working together with shared values and goals. They retained me to create a fee-based comprehensive financial, estate, and business succession plan. Their objective had always been to transition the business to Betty's daughter and Roger's two sons over time, but due to a series of unfortunate events, their dreams of keeping it in the family could not be realized. Betty was heartbroken, and Roger had an immediate need for liquidity. That's when I turned to ESG for ideas and support.

Dan: When you introduced me to Betty and Roger, we initiated our data gathering and financial statement review process. That culminated in our MARKETABILITY ASSESSMENT. We then introduced your owners to our construction industry specialist investment banking partners. They took our recommendation and hired the firm to pursue a sale of their business to an outside party. They chose this firm because of their construction expertise, buyer relationships, technical knowledge, and unique ability to consider and execute on a variety of exit paths. John and Matthew lead the team there. John, tell us about the journey.

John: Sure, Dan. We went to market but could not find an outside buyer that Betty and Roger felt was a good fit for their company culture. Furthermore, their management team, not thrilled about an outside deal, stepped up and said, "We want to buy it!" Betty and Roger were open to their request, so we thoroughly explored this route and discovered that a management buyout would not work because the team members lacked sufficient capital, weren't "bankable," and did not want to put their personal assets at risk. The team also did not want to place undue financial stress on the company with additional debt on the balance sheet. Cash flow was tight, and there was not a lot of headroom to protect the business if the construction market slowed down. In addition, the management team would have been using post-tax cash flow to service the debt, which is terribly inefficient and could lead to months (or years) of extra debt payments versus a levered employee stock option plan [ESOP] structure, which is highly tax-efficient. Neither side was happy with the management buyout scenario.

Matt: Without the management team on board, Betty and Roger were feeling frustrated and tinkered with the idea of just liquidating the company and its valuable heavy equipment to generate cash. However, we informed them that they had other options and that a liquidation would not only result in a loss of jobs and company legacy, but would also result in much less value received than what we deemed the fair market value of the company to be.

John: At that point we suggested the idea of an ESOP. Initially, Betty and Roger were skeptical, but only because they weren't fully aware of the numerous advantages of this strategy. That's when their astute financial advisor, Michael Cohen, stepped up to educate them on the benefits of an ESOP. He told them how it could accomplish their exit planning goals, reduce income taxes, provide a path to equity ownership for their key employees and others, and perpetuate the culture instilled in the company going forward. All that made this path a definite "go" for Betty and Roger. We shifted gears again, acting as intermediary to assist in the design and structure of the ESOP, introduce ESOP trustee candidates, negotiate all aspects of the transaction, obtain outside capital, and manage other aspects of the transaction process.

Dan: What special challenges did you have to address to make this ESOP happen, especially considering the pandemic?

Matt: Oh yes! In 2018, Congress passed legislation to make Small Business Administration [SBA] ESOP financing more practical. This transaction was one of the first, if not *the* first, to take advantage of the new legislation. Unfortunately, that meant we had to educate the SBA on the nuances of ESOPs, as they are quite different from what the SBA was accustomed to. We worked side by side with our lender and the SBA to navigate through, overcoming many obstacles around company cash flow and collateral and qualifying as a small business under the new rules. However, that was only the beginning: The ESOP transaction was scheduled to close by December 31, 2019, but we had to wait another two months for the SBA to approve the loan, then COVID-19 hit! As a result, the ESOP trustee pulled all deals they were working on.

Dan: You weren't alone on this one, Matt. The pandemic held up sales for a lot of owners, adding to the unprecedented disruption we all had to face. What happened next?

Matt: Fortunately, in March, the trustee came back and wanted to renegotiate the deal. We came to an agreement and set an August closing date. But there were more issues: The commercial banker we were dealing with was fired, so we had to find a replacement and get that person up to speed on SBA ESOP lending! In addition, the company had a Paycheck Protection Program [PPP] loan outstanding, and any change of control could endanger their eligibility for forgiveness. Finally, we needed consent from the SBA to sell to the ESOP with the PPP loan. In another stroke of fortune, along with some very focused work on our end, that was granted, and the transaction was approved and completed. We also helped with employment agreements for several key employees, as well as a lucrative incentive plan for the entire management team based on retention and performance of the company going forward.

Dan: I'm sure that was a relief for your owners! Mike, can you tell me more about the financial outcome and implementation?

Mike: Roger and Betty sold their company to the ESOP for approximately $10 million, of which they received half in cash at closing and half payable through a seller note receivable amortized over 10 years. With no prepayment penalty, we expect it actually will be paid to Roger and Betty sooner, in five to seven years. So far on our clients' behalf I have invested $2.6 million from the sale into a diversified actively managed portfolio and will add additional monies as Betty and Roger continue to get paid from the ESOP buyout. In addition, we rolled over Betty's 401(k) to an IRA to provide additional retirement income. We have placed life insurance and are talking about long-term care coverage. Most importantly, we satisfied Betty's and Roger's exit goals and maintained their company's outstanding culture.

> **"Betty and Roger were elated with the results on many levels. Not only were they pleased with the comprehensive service they received from our team; they also enjoyed the intangible benefits related to this win."**

Dan: That's excellent, Mike! I imagine Betty and Roger were very happy when the ESOP transaction closed?

Mike: They were elated with the results on many levels. Not only were they pleased with the comprehensive service they received from our team; they also enjoyed the intangible benefits related to this win. After the deal closed, they held a company meeting and handed each of their employees an envelope, telling everyone that information on the new owners could be found inside. After responding to a ceremonial "Please open the envelope," each of those assembled discovered it contained a mirror with a note that said "The new owner is you! Congratulations!!" That was quite a moment.

Dan: I love it! I'm sure it was an emotional moment for all. So, what's next for Betty and Roger?

Mike: Roger's proceeds paid off his debts and obligations, and he continues to work at the new company and is happy alongside his management team. Betty sits on the board and spends most of her time now on her 160-acre ranch, where she raises buffalo, enjoys her collection of classic cars, and cares for her child. Clearly, this was a win-win for everyone.

Key Takeaways

- Consider a variety of exit strategies and keep your options open. If your first choice turns out not to be feasible, your advisor can suggest another path that could be even more advantageous. Take on the unexpected and win!
- Work with a financial advisory team and investment banker who are objective and capable of changing course, if necessary.
- An ESOP can accomplish your exit planning goals, reduce income taxes, provide a path to equity ownership for your key employees and others, and perpetuate the culture instilled in your company going forward.

Chapter 15

Achieving Exit Success with a Management Team Buy-Out

Carl owned an industry-leading construction and design/build services firm. It was founded in the 1800s, and he took over in the early 1970s. The business was doing great, but facing court-ordered legal obligations and health issues, Carl needed liquidity—and quickly! That's when ESG and Sagemark Consulting Private Wealth Services Group collaborated to design an exit strategy that would accomplish all of Carl's goals. Challenges along the way threatened to disrupt the plan, but in the end, he was thrilled with the results: a key manager/employee purchase at a fair price. Another mission accomplished!

Objectives
- Satisfy an immediate need for liquidity.
- Owner originally yearned for family successor, but asked us to help him evaluate multiple exit paths: sale to outside buyers vs. a sale to their management team
- Ensure financial security during retirement.
- Consider the use of a charitable remainder trust to mitigate income and estate taxes.

Challenges
- Lack of a successor, mounting financial pressures, ongoing health concerns.
- Tight time frame to work within and a minimal amount of cash.

- Owner in 50/50 partnership with former spouse.
- Business objectives and family dynamics changed significantly during the process.
- General industry downturn left very few strategic companies in a position to acquire the company.

The ESG Team

- Dan Prisciotta, CFP®, CPA*, PFS, ChFC®, CBEC®, Managing Partner, Equity Strategies Group (ESG)
- Paul Meyer, CEPA, CBEC®, CRPC, BII Specialist, Sagemark Consulting Private Wealth Services
- Doug Richmond, CBEC®, BII Specialist and Director of Sagemark Consulting Private Wealth Services
- Dan W., Preferred ESG Investment Banker

Dan P: This all began with the courage of Paul Meyer, with Sagemark Consulting Private Wealth Services, who got up the nerve to cold-call Carl, a high-profile, affluent member of his community who served on a nonprofit board. Carl happened to own an industry-leading construction and design/build services firm that had been founded in the late 1800s, with him taking over in the 1970s. Paul had never met Carl, but empowered by the confidence instilled by Doug Richmond, director at Sagemark, he made the call and was able to schedule a face-to-face meeting with him. Paul, what transpired at that point?

Paul: We built a nice rapport almost immediately. He admitted that he had never had a comprehensive financial plan done to coordinate the many moving parts of his situation, and stated that given his pending divorce, it was an excellent time to consider our process, and he agreed to a next meeting.

Dan W: Carl seemed to be quite motivated.

Paul: Doug and I became immersed in the case and quickly learned the tremendous pressure Carl was under from his ex-wife and a serious medical condition worsened by stress. In addition to providing his personal guarantee for $50 million of bonding and a $5 million line of credit, he was a 50/50 partner in the construction management business and related real estate with his former spouse. Not only was his financial well-being at stake, but his second marriage was under fire. In addition, he had an obligation to maintain life insurance under a divorce decree and a desire to provide insurance for his new wife. The business had been in the family for four generations, and initially Carl's objective was definitely to pass it on to one of his sons, but now he needed liquidity.

Dan P: And that's where ESG came in.

Paul: That's right. Over the course of several months a lot changed, including family dynamics and business objectives, which effectively eliminated Carl's original family succession scenario. At that point Carl wanted to explore the immediate sale of his business, and that's when Doug and I knew it was time to contact ESG, whose capabilities had already been discussed early in our process. This is standard procedure for us when working with a business owner, even if they state they will never sell.

Dan P: Never say never! After introductions and an initial discussion, we got right to work. Carl and his management team fastidiously completed ESG's Valuation Planning Questionnaire. Carl embraced the ESG questionnaire and completed it with the help of his team. While many times business owners want this process very hush-hush, Carl actually wanted his team's input and insights. He realized that team members are talking about the future of the business even if the owner is not. They also wanted us to explore the viability of an S corporation ESOP, or a partial sale to their 50 employees, and use of a charitable remainder trust to mitigate taxes. This led to our analysis of corporate financial statements, operating agreements, organizational structure, and preparation of ESG's Marketability Assessment. Based on Carl's industry, the type and size of transaction desired, and other qualifying factors, we then introduced Carl to Dan W., one of our approved investment bankers with deep knowledge of his industry.

Dan W: Due to lack of a successor, mounting financial pressures, ongoing health concerns, and a loss of passion for the business, it was immediately clear to us that Carl needed a way out quickly, and that it would be a challenging path. He had a tight time frame to work within and a certain amount of cash that he needed to satisfy his planning needs. Within 24 hours, ESG and our firm held a teleconference with Carl, Doug, and Paul to present our recommendations. Carl certainly was very appreciative of our responsiveness and quick turnaround!

Paul: Carl was very impressed with our turnaround time, the level of detailed analysis, and the strength of our team. He had initially called a friend of his in the M&A world, and after nearly two weeks of waiting was wholly unimpressed. He stated more than once that he could not believe what we put together within 24 hours! We all needed to get up to speed quickly to work to achieve the timeline and cash goals. At this point, Carl felt that a sale to an outsider was his best option, which directed the case further into ESG's exit planning process. Carl doubted seriously that any of his management team had the risk tolerance to be an owner.

Dan P: While Carl had an attractive business, we knew that selling it would not be a cakewalk. Dan W. pointed out the challenges of the bonding requirements, and we all were aware that the construction industry was suffering through hard times. That left few strategic companies in a position to acquire, and even fewer private equity groups with an appetite for this company.

Dan W: All correct. Nevertheless, we accepted the challenge and proceeded with the creation of an offering memorandum and buyer list, identifying more than 150 potential strategic buyers and 200 private equity groups to approach.

Dan P: And off we went! Dan, how did the sales process proceed from there?

Dan W: Frankly, due to the size of the construction company, bonding, and debt, the response was unimpressive. In the midst of this, one of Carl's key managers emerged and expressed an interest in buying him out. Carl let us know that it would feel good to sell internally—that if he didn't take too much of a financial hit and if the key manager could obtain bank financing, he would seriously consider it.

Paul: So in the time that we had been working with Carl we went from a strong desire to pass it on to family, to a strong feeling that current management didn't have the risk appetite to be owners, to an internal transfer! Only because of our detailed holistic process and our deep understanding of our clients and their families and business associates did we make it happen. Dan W.'s expertise kicked in as he orchestrated the deal structure and negotiated with the bank to obtain SBA financing without requiring Carl's personal guarantee to provide acquisition funds and a line of credit to operate the business. The key manager acquired 75% of the company, and five other managers each ultimately acquired 5% stakes. Carl happily walked away with $5 million in cash proceeds from the sale, pulled out millions of excess cash from the corporate balance sheet, and will receive upside through an earnout based on future profitability. While he had to settle up with his ex-wife, he still emerged liquid and free of personal guarantees for $50 million of bonding and other debt!

Exit Planning—Inside and Out

The question of "Should I sell my business internally or to an outside buyer?" comes up all the time. If you think that transferring your business to your management team is inherently risky, you may be right. Inside transfers are risky because:

* Insiders typically have no money.
* Successors' management/ownership skills and commitment to ownership may be untested.
* You lose control of the business if you make the transfer before you are completely cashed out.

On the other hand, the possible benefits to this type of transfer include:

* Extending your legacy through your hand-picked management group.
* Motivating, retaining, and rewarding key employees.
* Retaining control until all, or most, of the purchase price is received.

◆ Remaining active in the business while gradually reducing your day-to-day responsibilities.

◆ Providing time for you to build up personal assets (via receipt of cash payments) before your exit.

It is key to design a plan that minimizes each risk so you can reap all of the potential benefits. Let's address each of these risks:

Insiders have no money, therefore it is too risky to sell to them.

This is true if you don't design a transfer strategy that puts money in their pockets as they increase the value of your company. Years in advance of the transfer, you will have to work steadily and effectively to build cash flow (the source for all cash out) through the installation of various value drivers to increase the value of your business and through careful planning to minimize taxation.

Unless you carefully plan to avoid it, cash flow can be taxed twice. This double tax (often totaling more than 50%) can spell disaster for many internal transfers. Through effective tax planning, however, some of this tax burden can be legally avoided.

Finally, you should use a modest, but defensible valuation for the company when transferring internally. Because a lower value is used for the purchase price, the size of the tax bite is correspondingly reduced. The difference between what you will receive from the sale of your business, at a lower price, and what you want to be paid after you leave the business is "made good" through a number of different techniques to extract cash from the company after you exit.

Successor's management/ownership skills are untested.

If that's the case, train your successors and create a written plan to systematically transition management and ownership responsibilities. During the transition period, you can test your assumptions and your successors' skills. This usually takes several years to complete.

You lose control before being cashed out.

This is only true if you fail to implement a transfer strategy designed to maintain control. In such a plan, you keep control through a well-designed and incremental sale of the company, over time, based upon improving company cash flow.

In summary, the keys to reduce the risks of an insider transfer are:

1. Plan the transfer well in advance of your desired exit date. Executing an insider transfer takes longer than executing a sale to a third party.
2. Value building activities are just as, if not more, important to an insider transfer as they are to a sale to a third party.
3. Plan design must be tax-sensitive.
4. The Plan must be in writing and make successors accountable.

Dan P: Impressive! We helped both the management team buyer and Carl to get the job done!

Paul: And he still has significant real estate holdings, which may be sold in the future. Thoroughly satisfied with our planning process, Carl has invested wisely and made numerous personal and professional introductions on behalf of Doug and me—and has been taking some well-deserved time off to enjoy life and go fishing with his son. We continue to work with Carl to keep his plan current, relevant, and sustainable.

Dan P: Great result, gentlemen! Kudos to you all for helping Carl achieve his vision of his ideal future, despite all of the hurdles he faced. Ongoing investment planning, insurance work, and estate and business planning continues to help Carl achieve current objectives. In fact, he continues to rely on us as part of his team to keep him financially organized, and we appreciate the opportunity for this great relationship.

Doug: It was our pleasure. In addition to a successful business exit, we helped Carl and his family by updating their estate plan and procuring $13 million of life insurance at an excellent rate (despite Carl's health challenges). I believe that the services ESG offers to Sagemark members during the planning process were key to our success here. It's a great feeling knowing our process truly helps people realize their dreams.

Key Takeaways

- It's not unusual for conditions to change during the course of marketing your company for exit.
- Rely on your professional advisors and be prepared to change course quickly and effectively to secure the ideal buyer.
- Even if you management team doesn't have the cash to buy you out, there may be creative ways to secure financing.
- Always bring up our extensive ESG capabilities, even (and especially) when your business owner clients say they will never sell.
- Embrace teamwork. The team that grew from Doug Richmond to Dan P. and ESG, and then Dan W., further strengthened the relationship with Carl.
- The transition of a company in this manner can help solidify multiple financial obligations and, even more importantly, relieve stress and allow the owner to focus more on family and health.
- Ongoing investment planning, insurance work, and estate and business planning will continue to help any owner achieve his or her ultimate objectives.

About the Author

Daniel A. Prisciotta CFP®, CPA*, PFS, ChFC®, CBEC®, founder and Managing Partner of Equity Strategies Group, is a well-known financial authority among privately owned middle market business owners. He is also the founder of Lincoln Financial Networks' Business Intelligence Institute (BII) and serves on its leadership committee. He has developed unique strategies to increase the value of businesses and to transfer businesses, either internally (to family or key employees) or externally (sale to outside buyers for the highest price). His previous books include *Defend Your Wealth: Protecting Your Assets in an Increasingly Volatile World* and *One Way Out: How to Grow, Protect, and Exit from Your Business.* Dan is a much sought-after speaker on the topics of business exit strategies and financial and estate planning, and has presented at numerous industry and association events. He has been interviewed numerous times on television and radio, and also quoted in *The Wall Street Journal, Fortune, Small Business,* and *The Los Angeles Times*. He is highly sought after by other financial professionals to collaborate and lend his expertise in planning for complex business situations.

With over 30 years of business exit, financial, and estate planning experience, Dan delivers a superior level of commitment and expertise necessary to create situation-based financial strategies and translate them into actionable steps.

Dan is always on the cutting edge of industry changes and innovations. He holds the following designations, certifications, and affiliations:

- Certified Business Exit Consultant (CBEC®)
- Certified Financial Planner™ (CFP®)
- Certified Public Accountant (CPA)*
- Personal Financial Specialist designation (PFS)
- Chartered Financial Consultant (ChFC®)
- American Institute of CPAs (AICPA)
- New Jersey Society of CPAs
- International Exit Planning Association (IEPA)
- National Association of Estate Planners & Councils (NAEPC)
- Society of Financial Service Professionals (SFSP)
- Financial Planning Association (FPA)
- Lifetime Member of the Resource Group
- Sagemark Consulting's Private Wealth Services Group
- Graduate of Brian Tracy's Advanced Speaker's Academy
- Registered Securities Principal and Representative
- Certified Continuing Education Instructor for CFP, PACE, CPA, CRPC, SFSP in multiple states

Dan is a Magna Cum Laude graduate of Fairleigh Dickinson University with a B.S. degree in Accounting, and resides in the New York City metro area.

Licensed, not practicing public accounting.

Disclaimer/Disclosure

This publication is designed to provide information about the subject matter covered. It is sold with the understanding that while the author is a financial advisor and registered representative, he, his firm, and the publisher are not engaged by the reader to render legal, accountant, or other professional services. The purpose of this book is to educate. Neither the author, nor Sagemark Consulting Private Wealth Services, nor Lincoln Financial Advisors, nor Equity Strategies Group, nor Daniel A. Prisciotta, shall have any liability or responsibility to any person or entity with respect to any loss or damage caused, or alleged to be caused, directly or indirectly by the information contained in this book. If you do not wish to be found by the above, you may return this book to the publisher for a full refund. Lincoln Financial Advisors Corporation and its representatives do not provide legal or tax advice. You may want to consult a legal or tax advisor regarding any legal or tax information as it relates to your personal circumstances. Securities offered through Lincoln Financial Advisors Corporation, a broker/dealer. Equity Strategies Group is the marketing name used to reflect specialized planning strategies and techniques. Investment advisory services offered through Sagemark Consulting, a division of Lincoln Financial Advisors Corporation, a registered investment advisor. Insurance offered through Lincoln Affiliates and other fine companies. Prisco Financial is not an affiliate of

Lincoln Financial Advisors. We provide critical, team attention for your financial planning needs that is difficult to match anywhere else.

Mergers and acquisitions (M&A) investment banking services are available through third-party firms not affiliated with Lincoln Financial Corp.

Index

V

W